Fodor's POCKET

copenhagen

D1361923

first edition

Excerpted from *Fodor's Denmark* and *Fodor's Sc...*

fodor's travel publications
new york • toronto • london • sydney • auckland
www.fodors.com

contents

maps

on the road with fodor's

THE MORE YOU KNOW BEFORE YOU GO, the better your trip will be. Copenhagen's most fascinating small museum (or its most stylish design store or chic restaurant) could be just around the corner from your hotel, but if you don't know it's there, it might as well be across the globe. That's where this guidebook and our Web site, Fodors.com, come in. Our editors work hard to give you useful, on-target information. Their efforts begin with finding the best contributors—people with good judgment and broad travel experience—the people you'd poll for tips yourself if you knew them.

Half-Danish and half-Spanish, **AnneLise Sørensen** grew up vacationing with her grandparents and cousins on Denmark's Jylland, where she was weaned on Farmor's *frikadellers* (grandmother's homemade Danish meatballs) and *smørrebrød* (open-face sandwiches). She currently divides her time between Europe and the U.S., where she writes and edits for various magazines and guidebooks. She has contributed to numerous Fodor's guides, including those to San Francisco, Ireland, and Spain. Her goals include writing a travel novella and mastering the pronounciation of that tricky guttural Danish ø in her last name.

Don't Forget to Write

Your experiences—positive and negative—matter to us. If we have missed or misstated something, we want to hear about it. We follow up on all suggestions. Contact the Pocket Copenhagen editor at editors@fodors.com or c/o Fodor's, 280 Park Avenue, New York, New York 10017. And have a fabulous trip!

Karen Cure
Editorial Director

Barents
Sea

COMMONWEALTH
OF INDEPENDENT
STATES
(RUSSIA)

Vardø

Vardø

Vadsø
Vadsö

Kirkenes

Utsjoki

Inari

Sodankylä

Kusamo

Pösio

Pudasjärvi

Puolanka

Suomussalmi

Kuhmo

Nurmes

Neets Cape

TO SVALBARD

Alta

Karasjok

Kautokeino

Ivalo

Kittilä

Kemijärvi

Rovaniemi

Kuhmo

Sotkamo

Kajaani

Kärsämäki

Nivala

Oulainen

Hammerfest

Enontekio

Muonio

Tornio

Kemi

Raahe

Pälikkila

Kalajoki

Kokkola

Umeå

Nurmes

Tornio

Torniojoki

Torneälv

Jokkmokk

Kalix

Piteå

Skellefteå

Gulf of Bothnia

Tromsø

Kilpisjärvi

Harstad

Narvik

Kiruna

Arvidsjaur

Arieplog

Åsele

Lycksele

Storuman

Sorsele

Tärnaby

Arctic Circle

Faukse

Bodø

Mo i Rana

Mosjøen

Vefsna

Namsos

Brønnøysund

Rørvik

Steinkjer

VESTRALEN

VALLFJORD

LOFOTEN

Sandnessjøen

Jostmealsälven

ATLANTIC OCEAN

Noruegian
Sea

200 miles

300 km

KEY

Ferry

Inset (ISLAND / ICELAND)

Arctic Circle

Raufarhöfn

Skagafjörður

Húsavík

Bakkafjöll

Vopnafjörður

Siglufjörður

Dalvík

Akureyri

Neskaupstaður

Egilsstaðir

Djúpivogur

Ísafjörður

Borðeyri

Blönduós

Breiðdalsvík

Þingeyri

Hofsjökull

Vatnajökull

Höfn

Fagurhólsmyri

Ýstfirðir

Búðardalur

Langjökull

Kirkjubæjarklaustur

Breiðafjörður

Borgafjörður

Búðir

Fellsfjall

Mýrdals-
jökull

Hella

Hyragerði

Hafnarfjörður

Stykkishólmur

Reykjavík

Vatnajökull

Westman Islands

ISLAND
(ICELAND)

TO ICELAND

denmark

SWEDEN

North Sea

Skagerrak

Kattegat

Anholt

Læsø

Aalborg Bugt

Skagen

Frederikshavn

Sæby

Grenå

Ebeltoft

Hirtshals

Hjørring

Aalborg

Randers

Århus

Samsø

Horsens

Brønderslev

Løkken

Hadsund

Viborg

Silkeborg

Skanderborg

Vejle

Thisted

Nykøbing

Skive

Jylland

Herning

Hanstholm

Lemvig

Struer

Holstebro

Ringkøbing

Grindsted

Skjern

Lim-fjord

Lim-fjord

Odden

Nykøbing

Frederikssund

Tisvildeje

Helsingør

Hornbæk

Hillerød

40

11

13

16

16

15

11

E45

TO GREENLAND

TO FAROE ISLANDS

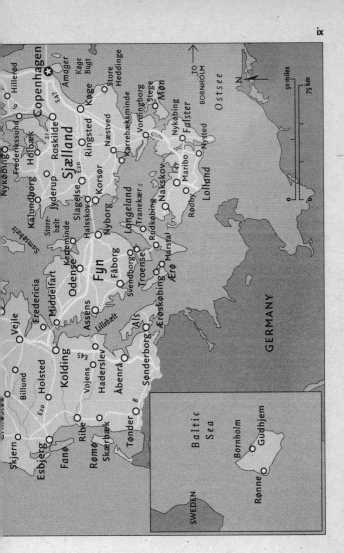

copenhagen

In This Chapter

introducing
copenhagen

COPENHAGEN—KØBENHAVN IN DANISH—HAS NO glittering skylines, few killer views, and only a handful of meager skyscrapers. Bicycles glide alongside manageable traffic at a pace that's utterly human. The early-morning air in the pedestrian streets of the city's core, Strøget, is redolent of freshly baked bread and soap-scrubbed storefronts. If there's such a thing as a cozy city, this is it.

Extremely livable and relatively calm, Copenhagen is not a microcosm of Denmark, but rather a cosmopolitan city with an identity of its own. Denmark's political, cultural, and financial capital is inhabited by 1.5 million Danes, a fifth of the national population, as well as a growing immigrant community. Filled with museums, restaurants, cafés, and lively nightlife, the city has its greatest resource in its spirited inhabitants. The imaginative, unconventional, and affable Copenhageners exude an egalitarian philosophy that embraces nearly all lifestyles and leanings.

The town was a fishing colony until 1157, when Valdemar the Great gave it to Bishop Absalon, who built a castle on what is now Christiansborg. It grew as a center on the Baltic trade route and became known as *købmændenes havn* (merchants' harbor) and eventually København. In the 15th century it became the royal residence and the capital of Norway and Sweden. A hundred years later, Christian IV, a Renaissance king obsessed with fine architecture, began a building boom that crowned the city with towers and castles, many of which still exist. They are almost all that remain of the city's 800-year history; much of Copenhagen was destroyed by two major fires in the 18th century and by Lord Nelson's bombings during the Napoleonic Wars.

Despite a tumultuous history, Copenhagen survives as the liveliest Scandinavian capital. With its backdrop of copper towers and crooked rooftops, the venerable city is amused by playful street musicians and performers, soothed by one of the highest standards of living in the world, and spangled by the thousand lights and gardens of Tivoli.

NEW AND NOTEWORTHY

The Øresund Bridge, one of Northern Europe's largest infrastructure projects, was completed in 2000. It links Denmark and Sweden across the 20-km (12-mi) Øresund Strait for the first time since the Ice Age ended 7,000 years ago. Consisting of a 4-km (2½-mi) underground tunnel (one of the longest in Europe), which connects via a man-made island to an 8-km (5-mi) bridge, the Øresund is an engineering marvel. For many Scandinavians, though, the bridge was not so much an engineering accomplishment as a cultural one. Malmö, Sweden's third-largest city, is now just a 35-minute train- or car-ride from Copenhagen. In traffic numbers, the bridge has been a success in its first year; more than double the amount of people cross the bridge daily than previously took the ferry. This number, however, has slowly been tapering off, and only time will tell whether the newly named Øresund region, headed by Copenhagen and Malmö, will grow into what many hope will be Scandinavia's new binational metropolis.

The stage for the Øresund Bridge had been set several years earlier by the building of the colossal Storebæltsbro (the Great Belt) rail and automobile link between Fyn and Sjælland, which reduced crossing times by at least an hour and eliminated, for better or worse, many of the enormous ferries that used to ply the Danish waters.

Streamlined travel between Copenhagen Airport and the city center should serve as a primer for urban planners everywhere: in good traffic, cars can zip from city center to the airport on the new highway in 20 minutes; the newest subway in the city train system can get you between the airport and the city's main train station in about 12. Copenhagen is now in the midst of building a new metro system, which will complement the extensive city S-train network. Scheduled to open in late 2002, the sleek metro trains will travel from Copenhagen's western suburbs to the city center, and then on to Amager, near the airport.

As Copenhagen continues to grow into Scandinavia's busiest conference capital, hotel capacity is increasing. Marriott unveiled its first Scandinavian hotel in late summer 2001, in Copenhagen: a five-star, 395-room harborfront property. The hotel boom will reach its zenith in 2003–2004, when no fewer than five new luxury hotels are opening up: they include a 400-room Rainbow Hotel near the airport, a 150-room First Hotel in the former Daells department store in the heart of town, and a new high-rise Scandic hotel alongside Tivoli.

PLEASURES AND PASTIMES

BIKING
Without a doubt, Denmark is one of the best places for biking. More than half the population pedals along city streets that effectively coordinate public transportation and cycle traffic, and along the country paths laced through Jylland and the island of Bornholm.

BOATING AND SAILING
Well-marked channels and nearby anchorages make sailing and boating easy and popular along the 7,300-km (4,500-mi)

coastline. In Copenhagen, the historic harbors of Christianshavn and Nyhavn and scores of marinas bristling with crisp, white sails are lined with old wooden houseboats, motorboats, yachts, and their colorful crews. And it's not only the well-heeled taking up this pastime: tousle-haired parents and babes, partying youths, and leathery pensioners tend to their boats and picnics, lending a festive, community spirit to the marinas.

DANISH DESIGN

Danish design has earned an international reputation for form and function. The best sales take place after Christmas and last until February; you can snatch up glassware, stainless steel, pottery, ceramics, and fur for good prices. Danish antiques and silver are also much cheaper here than in the United States. For major purchases—Bang & Olufsen products, for example—check prices stateside first so you can spot a good buy.

DINING

From the hearty meals of Denmark's fishing heritage to the inspired creations of a new generation of chefs, Danish cuisine combines the best of tradition and novelty. Though the country has long looked to the French as a beacon of gastronomy, chefs have proudly returned to the Danish table, emphasizing fresh, local ingredients and combining them with fusion trends. Many of Denmark's young, up-and-coming chefs are fully homegrown, completing all their training locally at the country's expanding list of superb, internationally recognized restaurants. Sample fresh fish and seafood from the Baltic; beef and pork from Jylland; and more-exotic delicacies, such as reindeer, caribou, seal meat, and whale from Greenland. Denmark's famed dairy products—sweet butter and milk among them—as well as a burgeoning organic foods industry, contribute to the freshness of the modern Danish kitchen.

Lunchtime is reserved for smørrebrød. You'll find the best, most traditional sampling of these open-face sandwiches in modest family-run restaurants that focus on generous—though never excessive—portions and artful presentation. If you fix your gaze on tender mounds of roast beef topped with pickles or baby shrimp piled high on a slice of French bread, you are experiencing a slice of authentic Danish culture. Another specialty is *wienerbrød*, a confection far superior to anything billed as "Danish pastry" elsewhere. The European flatfish plaice, which appears on many restaurant menus, is caught off the Scandinavian coast, and its mild meat goes well with many types of sauces (hence its popularity). All Scandinavian countries have versions of the cold table, but Danes claim that theirs, *det store kolde bord*, is the original and the best.

As for beer, the ubiquitous Carlsberg and Tuborg are facing international competition. But you can't do better than to stick with the Danish brands, which happily complement the traditional fare better than high-priced wine. For Christmas and Easter, Carlsberg and Tuborg release their perennially popular—and potent—Jul (Christmas) and Påske (Easter) brews. If you go for the harder stuff, try the famous *snaps*, the aquavit traditionally savored with cold food. For an evening tipple, have a taste of the uniquely Danish Gammel Dansk, a bitter that is consumed in small quantities.

LODGING

Accommodations in Copenhagen range from spare to splendid. Luxury hotels offer rooms of a high standard, and in a manor-house hotel you may find yourself sleeping in a four-poster bed. Even inexpensive hotels are well designed with good materials and good, firm beds—and Denmark's youth and family hostels are among the world's finest. Usually for all of July (and sometimes in the other summer months) conference hotels often lower prices and offer weekend specials.

In This Chapter

here and there

THE SITES IN COPENHAGEN RARELY JUMP OUT AT YOU; its elegant spires and tangle of cobbled one-way streets are best sought out on foot at an unhurried pace. Excellent bus and train systems can come to the rescue of weary legs. It is not divided into single-purpose districts; people work, play, shop, and live throughout the central core of this multilayered, densely populated capital.

Be it sea or canal, Copenhagen is surrounded by water. A network of bridges and drawbridges connects the two main islands—Sjælland and Amager—on which Copenhagen is built. The seafaring atmosphere is indelible, especially around Nyhavn and Christianshavn.

Some Copenhagen sights, especially churches, keep short hours, particularly in the fall and winter. It's a good idea to call directly to confirm opening times or check with the tourist offices.

Numbers in the text correspond to numbers in the margin and on the Copenhagen map

RÅDHUS PLADSEN, CHRISTIANSBORG SLOT, AND STRØGET

In 1728 and again in 1795, fires broke out in central Copenhagen with devastating effect. Disaster struck again in 1801, when Lord Nelson bombed the city—*after* the Danes had surrendered and *after* he was ordered to stop, he feigned ignorance and turned his famed blind eye to the command. These events still shape modern Copenhagen, which was rebuilt with wide, curved-corner streets—making it easier for fire trucks to turn—and large, four-side apartment buildings centered on courtyards. Arguably the liveliest area of the city, central Copenhagen is packed with shops, restaurants, businesses, and apartment buildings, as well as the crowning architectural achievements of Christian IV—all of it overflowing with Danes and visitors. Copenhagen's central spine consists of the five consecutive pedestrian strands known as Strøget and the surrounding tangle of roads and courtyards—less than a mile square in total. Across the capital's main harbor is the smaller, 17th-century Christianshavn. In the early 1600s, this area was mostly a series of shallows between land, which were eventually dammed. Today Christianshavn's colorful boats and postcard maritime character make it one of the toniest parts of town.

At this writing, the Dansk Jødisk Museum (Danish Jewish Museum) is on track to open near the Royal Library in the fall of 2002. Along with a general overview of Jewish history, it also will discuss in detail the Danish resistance movement, whose work during World War II helped bring nearly all of Denmark's 7,000 Jews to safety in Sweden.

A Good Walk

The city's heart is the Rådhus Pladsen, home to the baroque-style **RÅDHUS** ① and its clock tower. On the east side of the square is the landmark **LURBLÆSERNE** ②. Off the square's northeastern corner is Frederiksberggade, the first of the five pedestrian streets making up **STRØGET** ③, Copenhagen's shopping district. Walk northeast past the cafés and trendy boutiques to the double square of Gammeltorv and Nytorv.

Down Rådhusstræde toward Frederiksholms Kanal, the **NATIONALMUSEET** ④ contains an amazing collection of Viking artifacts. Cross Frederiksholms Kanal to Christiansborg Slotsplads, a small atoll divided by the canal and dominated by the burly **CHRISTIANSBORG SLOT** ⑤. North of the castle is **THORVALDSEN MUSEUM** ⑥, devoted to the works of one of Denmark's most important sculptors, Bertel Thorvaldsen. On the south end of Slotsholmen is the three-story Romanesque **KONGELIGE BIBLIOTEK** ⑦, edged by carefully tended gardens and tree-lined avenues. To the south, on the harbor side of the royal library, is its glass and granite annex, nicknamed the "Black Diamond." Back on the south face of Christiansborg are the **TEATERMUSEUM** ⑧ and the **KONGELIGE STALD** ⑨.

On the street that bears its name is the **TØJHUSMUSEET** ⑩, and a few steps away is the architecturally marvelous **BØRSEN** ⑪ and the **HOLMENS KIRKEN** ⑫. To the east is **CHRISTIANSHAVN**, connected to Slotsholmen by the drawbridge Knippelsbro. Farther north, the former shipyard of Holmen is marked by expansive venues and several departments of the Københavns Universitet.

From nearly anywhere in the area, you can see the green-and-gold spire of **VOR FRELSERS KIRKEN** ⑬. Across the Knippels Torvegade Bridge, about 1½ km (less than a mile) down Børgsgade through Højbroplads, is Amagertorv, one of Strøget's five streets. Here sits **W. Ø. LARSENS TOBAKMUSEET** ⑭, and farther down the street is the 18th-century **HELLIGÅNDS KIRKEN** ⑮. On Strøget's Østergade, the massive spire of **NIKOLAJ KIRKEN** ⑯ looks many sizes too large for the tiny cobble streets below.

TIMING

The walk itself takes about two hours. Typically, Christiansborg Slot and its ruins and the Nationalmuseet both take at least 1½ hours to see—even more for Viking fans. The hundreds of shops along Strøget are enticing, so plan extra shopping and café time—at least as much as your wallet can spare. Note that many attractions on this walk are closed Sunday or Monday, and some have odd hours; always call ahead or check with the tourist office.

copenhagen

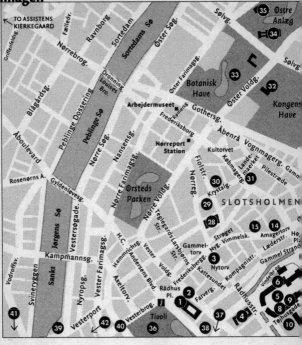

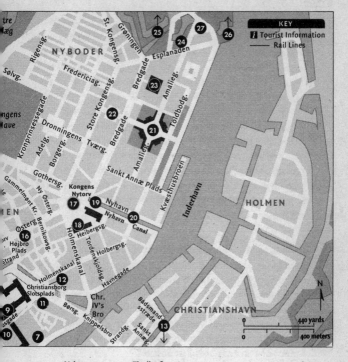

What to See

⑪ BØRSEN (Stock Exchange). This masterpiece of fantasy and architecture is the oldest stock exchange in Europe. The Børsen was built between 1619 and 1640, with the majority of construction in the 1620s. King Christian IV commissioned the building in large part because he wanted to make Denmark the economic superpower and crossroads of Europe. Rumor has it that when it was being built, he was the one who twisted the dragons' tails on the spire that tops the building. When it was first opened, it was used as a sort of medieval mall, filled with shopping stalls. Though parts of the Børsen still serve as an operating stock exchange, the bulk of the building houses the Chamber of Commerce, and therefore it's open only to accredited members and brokers. *Christiansborg Slotspl.*

OFF THE **CHRISTIANIA** – If you are nostalgic for the '60s counterculture,
BEATEN head to this anarchists' commune on Christianshavn. Founded
PATH in 1971, when students occupied army barracks, it is now a peaceful community of nonconformists who run a number of businesses, including a bike shop, bakery, rock club, and communal bathhouse. Wall cartoons preach drugs and peace, but the inhabitants are less fond of cameras—picture-taking is forbidden. *Prinsesseg. and Bådsmandsstr.*

★ ⑤ CHRISTIANSBORG SLOT (Christiansborg Castle). Surrounded by canals on three sides, the massive granite castle is where the queen officially receives guests. From 1441 until the fire of 1795, it was used as the royal residence. Even though the first two castles on the site were burned, Christiansborg remains an impressive baroque compound, even by European standards. At this writing tours of the free **Folketinget** (Parliament House; tel. 33/37–55–00) are given by appointment only. The assembly hall, where parliament members meet, may be open during their summer recess. At the **Kongelige Repræsantationlokaler** (Royal Reception Chambers), you're asked to don slippers to protect the floors. Admission is Dkr 40; entry is via guided tour only. Tours are given daily May through September, and Tuesday, Thursday, and weekends from October through April; English tours are at 11 and 3. The **Højesteret** (Supreme Court), on the site of the city's first fortress, was built by Bishop Absalon in 1167. The guards at the entrance are knowledgeable and friendly; call them first to double-check the court's complicated opening hours.

While the castle was being rebuilt around 1900, the Nationalmuseet excavated the **ruins** (tel. 33/92–64–92) beneath it. This dark, subterranean maze contains fascinating models and architectural relics. The ruins are open 9:30–3:30, daily May through September and Tuesday, Thursday, and weekends the rest of the year. Admission is Dkr 20.

Wander around **Højbro Plads** and the delightful row of houses that borders the northern edge of Slotsholmen. The quays here were long ago Copenhagen's fish market, but today most fresh fish is transported directly from boats to the city's fish shops and supermarkets. However, one lone fisherwoman still hawks fresh fish, marinated herring, and eel in the early morning. She is the last fishmonger you'll see carrying on the tradition. *Christiansborg.*

CHRISTIANSHAVN. Cobbled avenues, antique street lamps, and Left Bank charm make up one of the oldest neighborhoods in the city. Even the old system of earthworks—the best preserved of Copenhagen's original fortification walls—still exists. In the 17th century, King Christian IV offered what were patches of partially flooded land for free, and with additional tax benefits; in return, takers would have to fill them in and construct sturdy buildings for trade, commerce, housing for the shipbuilding workers, and defense against sea attacks. Gentrified today, the area harbors restaurants, cafés, and shops, and its ramparts are edged with green areas and walking paths, making it the perfect neighborhood for an afternoon or evening amble. The central square, Christianshavn Torv, is where all activity emanates from, and Torvegdage, a bustling shopping street, is the main thoroughfare. For a pleasant break, relax at one of the cafés along Wilders Canal, which streams through the heart of town.

⑮ HELLIGÅNDS KIRKEN (Church of the Holy Ghost). This 18th-century church was founded as an abbey of the Holy Ghost and is still one of the city's oldest places of worship. Its choir contains a font by the sculptor Thorvaldsen, and more-modern art is found in the large exhibition room—once a hospital—that faces Strøget. *Niels Hemmingseng. 5, Amagertorv section, no phone. Free. Weekdays 9–1, Sat. 10–noon.*

OFF THE BEATEN PATH **HOLMEN** – Previously isolated (indeed closed) from central Copenhagen, this former navy base just north of Christianshavn produced ships and ammunition until the 1980s. It was formally opened as the site of the 1995 United Nations Summit on Human Development and played an important role as a cultural area during Copenhagen's 1996 reign as the Cultural Capital of Europe. Today, among its several cultural venues is the city's biggest performance space, the Torpedo Hall, where torpedoes were actually produced. You'll also find the Danish Art Academy's Architecture School, the National Theater School, the Rhythmic Music Conservatory, and the Danish Film School, which all host special activities.

⑫ HOLMENS KIRKEN (Islet's Church). Two of the country's most revered naval heroes are buried here: Niels Juel crushed the Swedish fleet at Køge in 1677. Peder Tordenskjold defeated Charles XII of Sweden during the Great Northern War in the early 18th century. *Holmenskanal, tel. 33/12–95–55. Free. Mid-May–mid-Sept., weekdays 9–2 and Sat. 9–noon; mid-Sept.–mid-May, Mon.–Sat. 9–noon.*

❼ KONGELIGE BIBLIOTEK (Royal Library). The Royal Library houses the country's largest collection of books, newspapers, and manuscripts. Among the more than 2 million volumes are accounts of Viking journeys to America and Greenland and original manuscripts by Hans Christian Andersen and Karen Blixen (aka Isak Dinesen). If you happen to be in the area anyway, ramble around the statue of philosopher Søren Kierkegaard (1813–55), the formal gardens, and tree-lined avenues surrounding the scholarly building. The library's massive glass-and-granite annex, called the Black Diamond, looms between the main building and the waterfront. The Black Diamond hosts temporary historical exhibits that often feature books, manuscripts, and artifacts culled from the library's extensive holdings. The **National Museum of Photography,** also housed in the Black Diamond, contains a far-reaching collection of more than 25,000 Danish and international photographs. Temporary exhibits feature selections from the museum's collection. *Søren Kierkegaards Pl. 1, tel. 33/47– 47–47, www.kb.dk. Library free; admission varies for temporary exhibits. Library weekdays 10–7 and Sat. 10–2; exhibits Mon.–Sat. 10–7.*

NEED A BREAK? **OIEBLIKKET ESPRESSO BAR M.M.** (Søren Kierkegaards Pl. 1, tel. 33/47–49–50) operates out of a prime corner on the ground floor of the Royal Library's Black Diamond. The "m.m" in the name means "and more." It's named after a literary journal to which philosopher Søren Kierkegaard once contributed—and you too may be inspired to wax poetic as you gaze out over the canal and bask in the sunlight streaming through the soaring glass walls. In summer, the place sets up outdoor tables. (When summer the days turn nippy, you can sit in the snug indoors, while enjoying the effect of being outside, thanks to the natural light that floods in at all angles.) The simple fare includes croissants, brownies, and sandwiches made on fluffy round rolls.

❾ KONGELIGE STALD (Royal Stables). Between 9 and noon, time seems to stand still while riders, elegantly clad in breeches and jackets, exercise the horses. The vehicles, including coaches and carriages, and harnesses on display have been used by the Danish monarchy from 1778 to the present. *Christiansborg Ridebane 12, tel. 33/40–10–10. Dkr 10. May–mid-Oct., Fri.–Sun. 2–4; mid-Oct.–late Oct., Mon.–Thurs. 1–4, Fri.–Sun. 2–4; late Oct.–Apr., weekends 2–4.*

❷ LURBLÆSERNE (Lur Blower Column). Topped by two Vikings blowing an ancient trumpet called a lur, this column displays a good deal of artistic license—the lur dates from the Bronze Age, 1500 BC, whereas the Vikings lived a mere 1,000 years ago. City tours often start at this important landmark, which was erected in 1914. *East side of Rådhus Pl.*

★ ❹ NATIONALMUSEET (National Museum). This 18th-century royal residence, peaked by massive overhead windows, has housed what is regarded as one of the best national museums in Europe since the 1930s. Extensive collections chronicle Danish cultural history from prehistoric to modern times—included is one of the largest collections of Stone Age tools in the world—and Egyptian, Greek, and Roman antiquities are on display. The children's museum, with replicas of period clothing and all sorts of touchable items, transforms history into something to which children under age 12 can relate. *Ny Vesterg. 10, tel. 33/13–44–11, www.natmus.dk. Dkr 40; free Wed. Tues.–Sun. 10–5.*

⓰ NIKOLAJ KIRKEN (Nicholas Church). Though the green spire of the imposing church—named for the patron saint of seafarers—appears as old as the surrounding medieval streets, it is actually relatively young. The current building was finished in 1914; the previous structure, which dated from the 13th century, was destroyed by the 1728 fire. Today the church is an art gallery and exhibition center that often shows more-experimental work. *Nikolaj Pl., tel. 33/93–16–26. Varies according to special exhibitions. Daily noon–5.*

NEED A
BREAK? **CAFÉ NIKOLAJ** (Nikolajpl., tel. 33/93–16–26), inside Nikolaj
Kirken, is a reliable, inexpensive café with good pastries and
light meals. It's open noon to 3 for lunch and until 5 for cakes
and drinks.

① **RÅDHUS** (City Hall). Completed in 1905, the mock-Renaissance
building dominates **Rådhus Pladsen** (City Hall Square), the hub
of Copenhagen's commercial district. Architect Martin Nyrop's
creation was popular from the start, perhaps because he
envisioned that it should give "gaiety to everyday life and
spontaneous pleasure to all." A statue of Copenhagen's 12th-
century founder, Bishop Absalon, sits atop the main entrance.

Besides being an important ceremonial meeting place for
Danish VIPs, the intricately decorated Rådhus contains the
first **World Clock.** The multidial, superaccurate astronomical
timepiece has a 570,000-year calendar and took inventor Jens
Olsen 27 years to complete before it was put into action in 1955.
If you're feeling energetic, take a guided tour up the 350-ft bell
tower for the panoramic, but not particularly inspiring, view.

The modern glass and gray-steel **bus terminal** flanking the
square's northwest side has French granite floors, pear-tree-
wood shelving, and underground marble bathrooms. The $2.8
million creation proved so architecturally contentious—more
for its placement than for its design—that there was serious
discussion of moving it.

Look up to see one of the city's most charming bronze
sculptures, created by the Danish artist E. Utzon Frank in 1936.
Diagonally across Rådhus Pladsen, atop a corner office
building, are a **neon thermometer** and a **gilded barometer.** On
sunny days there's a golden sculpture of a girl on a bicycle; come
rain, a girl with an umbrella appears. *Rådhus Pl., tel. 33/66–25–
82. Tours Dkr 30, tower Dkr 20. Weekdays 9:30–4, Sat. 9:30–1. Tours
in English weekdays at 3, Sat. at 10 and 11. Tower tours June–Sept.,*

weekdays at 10, noon, and 2, Sat. at noon; Oct.–May, Mon.–Sat. at noon.

★ ③ **STRØGET.** Though it is referred to as one street, the city's pedestrian spine, pronounced Stroy-et, is actually a series of five streets: Frederiksberggade, Nygade, Vimmelskaftet, Amagertorv, and Østergade. By mid-morning, particularly on Saturday, it is congested with people, baby strollers, and street performers. Past swank and trendy, and sometimes flashy and trashy, boutiques of **Frederiksberggade** is the double square of **Gammeltorv** (Old Square) and **Nytorv** (New Square), in summer often crowded with street vendors selling cheap jewelry.

In 1728 and again in 1795, much of Strøget was heavily damaged by fire. When rebuilding, the city fathers straightened and widened the streets. You can still see buildings from this reconstruction period, as well as a few that survived the fires.

In addition to shopping, you can enjoy Strøget for strolling, as hundreds do. Outside the posh fur and porcelain shops and bustling cafés and restaurants, the sidewalks have a festive street-fair atmosphere.

⑧ **TEATERMUSEUM** (Theater Museum). After you brush up on theater and ballet history, wander around the boxes, stage, and dressing rooms of the **Royal Court Theater** of 1767, which King Christian VII had built as the first court theater in Scandinavia. *Christiansborg Ridebane 18, tel. 33/11–51–76. Dkr 20. Wed. 2–4, weekends noon–4.*

⑥ **THORVALDSEN MUSEUM.** The 19th-century artist Bertel Thorvaldsen (1770–1844) is buried at the center of this museum in a simple, ivy-covered tomb. Strongly influenced by the statues and reliefs of classical antiquity, he is recognized as one of the world's greatest neoclassical artists and completed many commissions all over Europe. The museum, once a coach house to Christiansborg, now houses Thorvaldsen's interpretations of classical and mythological figures, and an extensive collection of paintings and drawings by other artists that Thorvaldsen assembled while living—for most of his life—in Rome. The outside frieze by Jørgen Sonne depicts the sculptor's triumphant return to Copenhagen after years abroad. *Porthusg. 2, Slotsholmen, tel. 33/ 32–15–32, www.thorvaldsensmuseum.dk. Dkr 30. Tues.–Sun. 10–5.*

⑩ **TØJHUSMUSEET** (Royal Danish Arsenal Museum). This Renaissance structure—built by King Christian IV and one of central Copenhagen's oldest—contains impressive displays of uniforms, weapons, and armor in a 600-ft-long arched hall. *Tøjhusg. 3, tel. 33/11–60–37, www.thm.dk. Dkr 30. Tues.–Sun. noon–4.*

⑬ **VOR FRELSERS KIRKEN** (Church of Our Savior). Dominating the area around Christianshavn is the green-and-gold tower of this church, a baroque structure built in 1696. Local legend has it that the staircase encircling it was built curling the wrong way around, and that when its architect reached the top and realized what he'd done, he jumped. *Skt. Annæg. 29, tel. 32/57–27–98, www. vorfrelserskirke.dk. Tower Dkr 20. Apr.–Aug., Mon.–Sat. 11–4:30, Sun. noon–4:30; Sept.–Oct., Mon.–Sat. 11–3:30, Sun. noon–3:30. Tower closed in inclement weather.*

⑭ **W. Ø. LARSENS TOBAKMUSEET** (W. O. Larsens Tobacco Museum). The Tobacco Museum has a full-fledged collection of pipes made in every conceivable shape from every possible material. Look for the tiny pipe that's no bigger than an embroidery needle. There are also paintings, drawings, and an amazing collection of smoking implements. *Amagertorv 9, tel. 33/12–20–50. Free. Weekdays 10–6, Sat. 10–4.*

AROUND AMALIENBORG AND SITES NORTH

North of Kongens Nytorv, the city becomes a fidgety grid of parks and wider boulevards pointing northwest across the canal toward upscale Østerbro—wreathed by manors commissioned by wealthy merchants and blue bloods. In the mid-1700s, King Frederik V donated parcels of this land to anyone who agreed to build from the work of architect Niels Eigtved, who also designed the Kongelige Theater. The jewel of this crown remains Amalienborg and its rococo mansions.

A Good Walk

At the end of Strøget, **KONGENS NYTORV** ⑰ is flanked on its south side by the **KONGELIGE TEATER** ⑱, and backed by **CHARLOTTENBORG** ⑲, which contains the Danish Academy of Fine Art (call to see if an exhibition has opened the castle to the public). The street leading southeast from Kongens Nytorv is **NYHAVN** ⑳, a onetime sailors' haunt and now a popular waterfront hub. From the south end of the harbor (and the north end of Havnegade) high-speed craft leave for Malmö, Sweden; further north, Kvæsthusbroen—at the end of Skt. Annæ Plads— is the quay for boats to Oslo, Norway, and Bornholm, Denmark; further north still, just before the perch of The Little Mermaid, ships depart for Swinoujscie, Poland.

West of the harbor front is the grand square called Skt. Annæ Plads. Perpendicular to the square is Amaliegade, its wooden colonnade bordering the cobbled square of **AMALIENBORG** ㉑, the royal residence with a pleasant garden on its harbor side. Steps west from the square is Bredgade, where the baroque **MARMORKIRKEN** ㉒ flaunts its Norwegian marble structure. Farther north on Bredgade is the rococo **KUNSTINDUSTRIMUSEET** ㉓. Back on Bredgade (you can also take the more colorful, café-lined Store Kongensgade, just west), turn right onto Esplanaden and you'll see the enormously informative **FRIHEDSMUSEET** ㉔. At the Churchillparken's entrance stands the English church, St. Albans. In the park's center, the **KASTELLET** ㉕ serves as a reminder of the city's grim military history. At its eastern perimeter is Langelinie, a waterfront promenade with a view of Denmark's best-known pinup, **DEN LILLE HAVFRUE** ㉖. Wending your way back toward Esplanaden and the town center, you'll pass the **GEFION SPRINGVANDET** ㉗.

TIMING

This walk amid parks, gardens, canals, and building exteriors should take a full day. If the weather is nice, linger in the parks, especially along Kastellet and Amalienhaven, and plan on a long lunch at Nyhavn. The Kunstindustrimuseet merits about an hour, more if you plan on perusing the design books in the museum's well-stocked library. The Frihedsmuseet may require more time: its evocative portrait of Danish life during World War II intrigues even the most history-weary teens. Avoid taking this tour Monday, when some sites are closed.

What to See

㉑ **AMALIENBORG** (Amalia's Castle). The four identical rococo buildings occupying this square have housed the royals since 1784. The Christian VIII palace across from the Queen's residence houses the **Amalienborg Museum,** which displays the second division of the Royal Collection (the first is at Rosenborg Slot) and chronicles royal lifestyles between 1863 and 1947. Here you can view the study of King Christian IX (1818–1906) and the drawing room of his wife, Queen Louise. Rooms are packed with family gifts and regal baubles ranging from tacky knickknacks to Fabergé treasures, including a nephrite-and-ruby table clock, and a small costume collection.

In the square's center is a magnificent equestrian statue of King Frederik V by the French sculptor Jacques François Joseph Saly. It reputedly cost as much as all the buildings combined. Every day at noon, the Royal Guard and band march from Rosenborg Slot through the city for the changing of the guard. At noon on Queen Margrethe's birthday, April 16, crowds of Danes gather to cheer their monarch, who stands and waves from her balcony. On Amalienborg's harbor side are the trees, gardens, and fountains of **Amalienhaven**. *Amaliego., tel. 33/12–21–86. Dkr 40. May–Oct., daily 10–4; Nov.–Apr., Tues.–Sun. 11–4.*

CHARLOTTENBORG (Charlotte's Castle). This Dutch baroque-style castle was built by Frederik III's half brother in 1670. Since 1754 the garden-flanked property has housed the faculty and students of the Danish Academy of Fine Art. It is open only during exhibits, usually in winter. *Nyhavn 2, tel. 33/13–40–22, www.charlottenborg-art.dk. Dkr 20. During exhibitions, daily 10–5 (Wed. until 7).*

DEN LILLE HAVFRUE (The Little Mermaid). On the Langelinie promenade, this somewhat overhyped 1913 statue commemorates Hans Christian Andersen's lovelorn creation, and is the subject of hundreds of travel posters. Donated to the city by Carl Jacobsen, the son of the founder of Carlsberg Breweries, the innocent waif has also been the subject of some cruel practical jokes, including decapitation and the loss of an arm, but she is currently in one piece. Especially on a sunny Sunday, the Langelinie promenade is thronged with Danes and visitors making their pilgrimage to see the statue. On this occasion, you may want to read the original Hans Christian Andersen tale; it's a heart-wrenching story that's a far cry from the Disney cartoon.

FRIHEDSMUSEET (Resistance Museum). Evocative, sometimes moving displays commemorate the heroic Danish resistance movement, which saved 7,000 Jews from the Nazis by hiding and then smuggling them to Sweden. The homemade tank outside was used to spread the news of the Nazi surrender after World War II. *Churchillparken, tel. 33/13–77–14, www.natmus.dk. Dkr 40, free Wed. May–mid-Sept., Tues.–Sat. 10–4, Sun. 10–5; mid-Sept.–Apr., Tues.–Sat. 11–3, Sun. 11–4.*

GEFION SPRINGVANDET (Gefion Fountain). Not far from The Little Mermaid yet another dramatic myth is illustrated. The goddess Gefion was promised as much of Sweden as she could carve in a night. She changed her sons to oxen and used them to portion off what is now the island of Sjælland. The statue shows them all hard at work. *East of Frihedsmuseet.*

㉕ KASTELLET (Citadel). At Churchill Park's entrance stands the spired English church **St. Albans.** From there, walk north on the main path to reach the Citadel. The structure's smooth, peaceful walking paths, marina, and greenery belie its fierce past as a city fortification. Built in the aftermath of the Swedish siege of the city on February 10, 1659, the double moats were among the improvements made to the city's defense. The Citadel served as the city's main fortress into the 18th century; in a grim reversal during World War II, the Germans used it as headquarters during their occupation. *Center of Churchill Park. Free. Daily 6 AM–sunset.*

⑱ KONGELIGE TEATER (Danish Royal Theater). The stoic, pillared and gallery-fronted theater is the country's preeminent venue for music, opera, ballet, and theater. The Danish Royal Ballet performs here; its repertoire ranges from classical to modern works.

The current building was opened in 1874, though the annex, known as the **Nesting Box,** was not inaugurated until 1931. Statues of Danish poet Adam Oehlenschläger and author Ludvig Holberg—whose works remain the core of Danish theater—flank the facade. Born in Bergen, Norway, in 1684, Holberg came to Denmark as a student and stayed. Often compared to Molière, he wrote 32 of his comedies in a "poetic frenzy" between 1722 and 1728, and, legend has it, he complained of interminable headaches the entire time. He published the works himself, made an enormous fortune, and invested in real estate. In the mid-'90s, an annex designed by Norwegian architect Sverre Fehn was planned for construction on the eastern side of the theater, but those plans—indeed the whole expansion—are now being reconsidered. *Tordenskjoldsg. 3, tel. 33/69–69–69. Guided tours 75 Dkr. Guided tours Sun. 11; no tours May 27–Aug. 5.*

★ **⑰ KONGENS NYTORV** (King's New Square). A mounted statue of Christian V dominates the square. Crafted in 1688 by the French sculptor Lamoureux, the subject is conspicuously depicted as a Roman emperor. Every year, at the end of June, graduating high school students arrive in horse-drawn carriages and dance beneath the furrowed brow of the sober statue. *Between Gothersg., Holmenskanal, and Heibergsg.*

NEED A BREAK? Dozens of restaurants and cafés line Nyhavn. Among the best is **CAP HORN** (Nyhavn 21, tel. 33/12–85–04), for moderately priced and completely organic Danish treats served in a cozy, art-filled dining room that looks like a ship's galley. Try the fried plaice, swimming in a sea of parsley butter with boiled potatoes. In the summertime, try to grab a sidewalk table, the perfect place to enjoy an overstuffed focaccia sandwich and a Carlsberg.

㉓ KUNSTINDUSTRIMUSEET (Museum of Decorative Art). Originally built in the 18th century as a royal hospital, the fine rococo museum houses a large selection of European and Asian crafts. Also on display are ceramics, silverware, tapestries, and special exhibitions that usually focus on contemporary design. The museum's excellent library is stocked with design books and magazines. A small café also operates here. *Bredg. 68, tel. 33/14–94–52. Dkr 35 (additional fee for some special exhibits). Permanent collection, Tues.–Fri. 1–4, weekends noon–4; changing exhibits, Tues.–Fri. 10–4, weekends noon–4.*

㉒ MARMORKIRKEN (Marble Church). Officially the Frederikskirke, this ponderous baroque sanctuary of precious Norwegian marble was begun in 1749 and remained unfinished from 1770 to 1874 due to budget restraints. It was finally completed and consecrated in 1894. Around the exterior are 16 statues of various religious leaders from Moses to Luther, and below them stand sculptures of outstanding Danish ministers and bishops. The hardy can scale 273 steps to the outdoor balcony. From here you can walk past the exotic gilded onion domes of the **Russiske Ortodoks Kirke** (Russian Orthodox Church). *Bredg., tel. 33/15–37–63. Free; balcony Dkr 20. Mon.–Tues. and Thurs.–Sat. 10:30–4:30; Wed. 10:30–6. Guided tours: Aug.–May, weekends at 1; June–July, daily at 1 and 3.*

★ ⑳ **NYHAVN** (New Harbor). This harbor-front neighborhood was built 300 years ago to attract traffic and commerce to the city center. Until 1970, the area was a favorite haunt of sailors. Though restaurants, boutiques, and antiques stores now outnumber tattoo parlors, many old buildings have been well preserved and have retained the harbor's authentic 18th-century maritime atmosphere; you can even see a fleet of old-time sailing ships from the quay. Hans Christian Andersen lived at various times in the Nyhavn houses at numbers 18, 20, and 67.

DOWN NØRREBRO

By the 1880s, many of the buildings that now line Nørrebro were being hastily thrown up as housing for area laborers. Many of these flats—typically decorated with a row of pedimented windows and a portal entrance—have been renovated through a massive urban-renewal program. But to this day, many share hall toilets, have no showers, and are heated only by kerosene heaters. On the Nørrebrogade and Skt. Hans Torv of today, you'll discover a fair number of cafés, restaurants, clubs, and shops.

A Good Walk

Take the train from Østerport Station, off of Oslo Plads, to Nørreport Station on Nørre Voldg. and walk down Fiolstræde to **VOR FURE KIRKEN** ㉘. The church's very tall copper spire and four shorter ones crown the area. Backtrack north on Fiolstræde, to the main building of **KØBENHAVNS UNIVERSITET** ㉙; on the corner of Krystalgade is the **KØBENHAVNS SYNAGOGE** ㉚.

Fiolstræde ends at the Nørreport train station. Perpendicular to Nørrevoldgade is Frederiksborggade, which leads northwest to the neighborhood of Nørrebro; to the south after the Kultorvet, or Coal Square, Frederiksborggade turns into the pedestrian street Købmagergade. From anywhere in the area, you can see the stout **RUNDETÅRN** ㉛: the round tower stands as one of

Copenhagen's most beloved landmarks, with an observatory open on autumn and winter evenings. Straight down from the Rundetårn on Landemærket, Gothersgade gives way to **ROSENBORG SLOT** ㉜, its Dutch Renaissance design standing out against the vivid green of the well-tended Kongens Have. For a heavier dose of plants and living things, head across Øster Voldgade to the 25-acre **BOTANISK HAVE** ㉝. South of the garden is the Arbejdermuseet (Worker's Museum), which profiles the lives of workers from the late 1800s to the present.

Leave the garden's north exit to reach the **STATENS MUSEUM FOR KUNST** ㉞, notable for exceptional Matisse works. An adjacent building houses the **HIRSCHSPRUNGSKE SAMLING** ㉟, with 19th-century Danish art. Near here, on the east side of Øster Voldgade, is Nyboder, a neighborhood full of tidy homes for sailors that were built by Christian IV.

TIMING

All of the sites on this tour are relatively close together and can be seen in roughly half a day. Note that some sites close Monday or Tuesday; call ahead. The tour can be easily combined with the one that follows—just head back to Nørreport station and catch a train to Hovedbanegården.

What to See

ARBEJDERMUSEET. The vastly underrated Workers' Museum chronicles the working class from 1870 to the present, with evocative life-size "day-in-the-life-of" exhibits, including reconstructions of a city street and tram and an original apartment once belonging to a brewery worker, his wife, and eight children. Changing exhibits focusing on Danish as well as international issues are often excellent. The museum also has a 19th-century–style restaurant serving old-fashioned Danish specialties and a '50s–style coffee shop. Rømersg. 22, tel. 33/93–25–75, www.arbejdermuseet.dk. Dkr 50. July–Oct., daily 10–4; Nov.–June, Tues.–Sun. 10–4.

OFF THE **ASSISTENS KIERKEGAARD** – (Assistens Cemetery). This
BEATEN peaceful, leafy cemetery in the heart of Nørrebro is the final
PATH resting place of numerous great Danes, including Søren
Kierkegaard (whose last name means "church garden," or
"cemetery"), Hans Christian Andersen, and physicist Niels
Bohr. In the summer, the cemetery takes on a cheerful, city-park
air as picnicking families, young couples, and sunbathers relax
on the sloping lawns amid the dearly departed. *Kapelvej 2, tel. 35/
37–19–17. Free. May–Aug., daily 8–8; Sept.–Oct., daily 8–6; Nov.–
Apr., daily 8–4.*

③③ BOTANISK HAVE (Botanical Garden). Trees, flowers, ponds,
sculptures, and a spectacular 19th-century Palmehuset (Palm
House) of tropical and subtropical plants blanket the garden's
25-plus acres. There's also an observatory and a geological
museum. Take time to explore the gardens and watch the
pensioners feed the birds. Some have been coming here so long
that the birds actually alight on their fingers. *Gothersg. 128, tel. 35/
32–22–40, www.botanic-garden.ku.dk. Free. Gardens May–Sept., daily
8:30–6; Oct.–Apr., Tues.–Sun. 8:30–4; Palm House daily 10–3.*

③⑤ HIRSCHSPRUNGSKE SAMLING (Hirschsprung Collection). This
museum showcases paintings from the country's Golden Age—
Denmark's mid-19th-century school of Naturalism—as well as a
collection of paintings by the late-19th-century artists of the
Skagen School. Their luminous works capture the play of light and
water so characteristic of the Danish countryside. *Stockholmsg. 20,
tel. 35/42–03–36, www.hirschsprung.dk. Dkr 25. Thurs.–Mon. 11–4,
Wed. 11–9.*

③⓪ KØBENHAVNS SYNAGOGE (Copenhagen Synagogue). The
contemporary architect Gustav Friedrich Hetsch borrowed from
the Doric and Egyptian styles in creating this arklike synagogue.
Krystalg. 12. Daily services 4:15.

②⑨ KØBENHAVNS UNIVERSITET (Copenhagen University).
Denmark's leading school for higher learning was constructed

in the 19th century on the site of the medieval bishops' palace. Nørreg. 10, tel. 35/32–26–26.

NEED A BREAK?
Near Copenhagen University is **SØMODS BOLCHER** (Nørreg. 36, tel. 33/12–60–46), a must for children and candy lovers: its old-fashioned hard candy is pulled and cut by hand.

NYBODER. Tour the neat, mustard-color enclave of Nyboder, a perfectly laid-out compound of flat, long, former sailors' homes built by Christian IV. Like Nyhavn, the area was seedy and boisterous at the beginning of the 1970s, but today has become one of Copenhagen's more fashionable neighborhoods. Stroll by on your own or call to make arrangements to visit one of the houses (ask for Mr. Timler). *West of Store Kongensg. and east of Rigensg., tel. 33/32–10–05.*

★ 32 **ROSENBORG SLOT** (Rosenborg Castle). This Dutch Renaissance castle contains ballrooms, halls, and reception chambers, but for all of its grandeur, there's an intimacy that makes you think the king might return any minute. Thousands of objects are displayed, including beer glasses, gilded clocks, golden swords, family portraits, a pearl-studded saddle, and gem-encrusted tables; an adjacent treasury contains the royal jewels. The castle's setting is equally welcoming: it's in the middle of the **Kongens Have** (King's Garden), amid lawns, park benches, and shady walking paths.

King Christian IV built the Rosenborg Castle as a summer residence but loved it so much that he ended up living and dying here. In 1849, when the absolute monarchy was abolished, all the royal castles became state property, except for Rosenborg, which is still passed down from monarch to monarch. Once a year, during the fall holiday, the castle stays open until midnight, and visitors are invited to explore its darkened interior with bicycle lights. *Øster Voldg. 4A, tel. 33/15–32–86. Dkr 50. Jan.–May and Nov.–mid-Dec., Tues.–Sun. 11–2; June, daily 10–4; July–Sept., daily 10–5; Oct., daily 11–3.*

★ ③ **RUNDETÅRN** (Round Tower). Instead of climbing the stout Round Tower's stairs, visitors scale a smooth, 600-ft spiral ramp on which—legend has it—Peter the Great of Russia rode a horse alongside his wife, Catherine, who took a carriage. From its top, you enjoy a panoramic view of the twisted streets and crooked roofs of Copenhagen. The unusual building was constructed as an observatory in 1642 by Christian IV and is still maintained as the oldest such structure in Europe.

The art gallery has changing exhibits, and occasional concerts are held within its massive stone walls. An observatory and telescope are open to the public evenings mid-October through March, and an astronomer is on hand to answer questions. *Købmagerg. 52A, tel. 33/73–03–73, www.rundetaarn.dk. Dkr 15. June–Aug., Mon.–Sat. 10–8, Sun. noon–8; Sept.–May, Mon.–Sat. 10–5, Sun. noon–5. Observatory and telescope mid-Oct.–Mar., Tues.–Wed. 7 PM–10 PM.*

③ **STATENS MUSEUM FOR KUNST** (National Art Gallery). Old Master paintings—including works by Rubens, Rembrandt, Titian, El Greco, and Fragonard—as well as a comprehensive array of old and 20th-century Danish art make up the gallery collection. Also very notable is the modern foreign art, which includes pieces by a very small but select group of artists, including Henri Matisse, Edvard Munch, Henri Laurens, Emil Nolde, and Georges Braque. The space also includes a children's museum, an amphitheater, a documentation center and study room, a bookstore, and a restaurant. A sculpture garden filled with classical, modern, and whimsical pieces flanks the building. *Sølvg. 48–50, tel. 33/74–84–94, www.smk.dk. Dkr 40; free Wed. Tues. and Thurs.–Sun., 10–5; Wed. 10–8.*

② **VOR FURE KIRKEN** (Church of Our Lady). Copenhagen's cathedral since 1924 occupies a site that has drawn worshipers since the 13th century, when Bishop Absalon built a chapel here. Today's church is actually a reconstruction: the original church was destroyed during the Napoleonic Wars. Five towers top the neoclassical structure. Inside you can see Thorvaldsen's marble sculptures depicting Christ and the 12 Apostles, and Moses and David, cast in bronze. Nørreg., Frue Pl., tel. 33/15–10–78. Free. Mon.–Sat. 9–5, Sun. noon–4:30. (On Fri. the church usually closes 10–noon.) Oct.–Mar., hrs vary on Sun., so call ahead.

OFF THE
BEATEN
PATH
ZOOLOGISKE HAVE – Many children love the Zoological Gardens, home to more than 2,000 animals. The small petting zoo and playground includes cows, horses, rabbits, goats, and hens. The indoor rain forest has butterflies, sloths, alligators, and other tropical creatures. Sea lions, lions, and elephants are fed in the early afternoon. Be warned: on sunny weekends, the line to enter runs far down Roskildevej; get here early. Roskildevej 32, tel. 36/30–20–01, www.zoo.dk. Dkr 70. June–Aug., daily 9–6; Sept.–Oct. and Apr.–May, daily 9–5; Nov.–Mar., daily 9–4.

IN AND AROUND VESTERBROGADE

To the southwest of the city are the vibrant working-class and immigrant neighborhoods of Vesterbro, where you'll find a good selection of inexpensive ethnic restaurants and shops. Like the area around Nørrebro, the buildings date from the late 1800s and were constructed for workers.

A Good Walk

Begin your tour from Copenhagen's main station, Hovedbanegården. When you exit on Vesterbrogade, take a right and you can see the city's best-known attraction, **TIVOLI** ㊱. At the southern end of the gardens, on Hans Christian Andersens Boulevard, the neoclassical **NY CARLSBERG GLYPTOTEK** ㊲ contains one of the most impressive collections of antiquities and sculpture in northern Europe. Just north on Hans Christian Andersens Boulevard, across the street from Tivoli's eastern side, is the sleek **DANSK DESIGN CENTER** ㊳, with innovative temporary exhibits that showcase Danish and international design. To the west of the main station and tucked between Sankt Jørgens Sø, or St. Jørgens Lake, and the main arteries of Vestersøgade and Gammel Kongevej is the **TYCHO BRAHE PLANETARIUM** ㊴, with an Omnimax Theater.

VESTERBRO ㊵, which resembles the New York's Lower East Side for its bohemian vibe and ethnically diverse population, is along Vesterbrogade near Tivoli. Parallel to the south is **ISTEDGADE**, Copenhagen's half-hearted red-light district.

Farther west on Vesterbrogade is **KØBENHAVNS BYMUSEUM** ㊶, its entrance flanked by a miniature model of medieval Copenhagen. Beer enthusiasts can head south on Enghavevej and take a right on Ny Carlsbergvej to see the **CARLSBERG BRYGGERI** ㊷. The visitor's center, nearby, on Gamle Carslbergvej, has exhibits on the brewing process and Carlsberg's rise to fame.

TIMING
These sights can be seen in half a day, and could be combined easily with a walk around Nørrebo. Tivoli offers charms throughout the day; visit in the late afternoon, and stay until midnight, when colored electrical bulbs and fireworks illuminate the park. Be sure to call ahead, since some places may be closed on Monday or Tuesday.

What to See

㊷ **CARLSBERG BRYGGERI** (Carlsberg Brewery). As you approach the world-famous Carlsberg Brewery, the unmistakable smell of fermenting hops greets you, a pungent reminder that this is beer territory. (Indeed, near the Brewery is the appealing little neighborhood of Humleby; "humle" means "hops.") Four giant Bornholm granite elephants guard the brewery's main entrance on Ny Carlsbergvej. Nearby, on Gamle Carlsbergvej, is the visitor's center, in an old Carlsberg brewery. Colorful displays take you step by step through the brewing process. You can also walk through the draft horse stalls; at the end of your visit, you're rewarded with a few minutes to quaff a complimentary beer. The free **Carlsberg Museum** (Valby Langgade 1, tel. 33/27–12–74), open Tuesday through Sunday 10–3, offers a further look into the saga of the Carlsberg family, and how it managed to catapult Carlsberg from a local name into one of the most famous beers in the world. *Gamle Carlsbergvej 11, tel. 33/27–13–14, www.carlsberg.dk. Free. Tues.–Sun. 10–4.*

38 DANSK DESIGN CENTER (Danish Design Center). This sleek, glass-panel structure looms in sharp contrast to the old-world ambience of Tivoli just across the street. More of a design showroom than a museum, the center's highlights are the innovative temporary exhibits on the main floor. Past exhibits have included "75 years of Bang & Olufsen," which covered the the famed Danish audio-system company, and "Tooltoy," a playful, interactive exhibit of toys over the last century. One-third of the temporary exhibits showcase Danish design; the rest focus on international design. The semi-permanent collection on the ground floor (renewed every other year) often includes samples from the greats, including chairs by Arne Jacobsen, several artichoke PH lamps (designed by Poul Henningsen), and Bang & Olufsen radios and stereos. Note how even the radios they made in the '50s look more modern than many of the radios today. The center's shop carries a wide range of Danish design items and selected pieces from the temporary exhibits. You can enjoy light meals in the atrium café, sitting amid the current exhibits. *H.C. Andersens Blvd. 27, tel. 33/69–33–69, www.ddc.dk. Dkr 30. Weekdays 10–5, weekends 11–4.*

ISTEDGADE. In what passes for a red-light district in Copenhagen, mom-and-pop kiosks and ethnic restaurants stand side by side with porn shops and shady outfits aiming to satisfy all proclivities. Istedgade, like its neighboring street Vesterbrogade, has been diversifying over the past several years, drawing artists and students. Thanks to the city's urban-renewal projects, new cafés and businesses are also moving in, mostly on the southwest end of Istedgade, around Enghave Plads (Enghave Square). Mama Lustra, at No. 96–98, is a laid-back café with comfy armchairs and a mixed crowd of students and older artsy types. Though Istedgade is relatively safe, you may want to avoid the area near the Central Station late at night. *South and parallel to Vesterbrogade, west of Tivoli.*

41 KØBENHAVNS BYMUSEUM (Copenhagen City Museum). For a surprisingly evocative collection detailing Copenhagen's history, head to this 17th-century building in the heart of Vesterbro. Outside is a meticulously maintained model of medieval Copenhagen; inside there is also a memorial room for philosopher Søren Kierkegaard, the father of existentialism. *Vesterbrog. 59, tel. 33/21–07–72, www.kbhbymuseum.dk. Dkr 20, free Fri. May–Sept., Wed.–Mon. 10–4; Oct.–Apr., Wed.–Mon. 1–4.*

★ **37 NY CARLSBERG GLYPTOTEK** (New Carlsberg Museum). Among Copenhagen's most important museums—thanks to its exquisite antiquities and Gauguins and Rodins—the neoclassical New Carlsberg Museum was donated in 1888 by Carl Jacobsen, son of the founder of the Carlsberg Brewery. Surrounding its lush indoor garden, a series of nooks and chambers houses works by Degas and other impressionists, plus an extensive assemblage of Egyptian, Greek, Roman, and French sculpture, not to mention Europe's finest collection of Roman portraits and the best collection of Etruscan art outside Italy. A modern wing, designed as a three-story treasure chest by the acclaimed Danish architect Henning Larsen, houses an impressive pre-impressionist collection that includes works from the Barbizon school; impressionist paintings, including works by Monet, Alfred Sisley, and Pissarro; and a postimpressionist section, with 50 Gauguin paintings plus 12 of his very rare sculptures. *Dantes Pl. 7, tel. 33/41–81–41, www.glyptoteket.dk. Dkr 30, free Wed. and Sun. Tues.–Sun. 10–4.*

★ ☙ **36 TIVOLI.** Copenhagen's best-known attraction, conveniently next to its main train station, attracts an astounding number of visitors: 4 million people from mid-April through September. Tivoli is more sophisticated than a mere amusement park: among its attractions are a pantomime theater; open-air stage; 24 restaurants (some of them quite elegant); and frequent classical, jazz, and rock concerts. Fantastic flower exhibits color the lush gardens and float on the swan-filled ponds.

The park was established in the 1840s, when Danish architect George Carstensen persuaded a worried King Christian VIII to let him build an amusement park on the edge of the city's fortifications, rationalizing that "when people amuse themselves, they forget politics." On Wednesday and weekend nights, elaborate fireworks are set off, and every day the Tivoli Guard, a youth version of the Queen's Royal Guard, performs. Try to see Tivoli at least once by night, when 100,000 colored lanterns illuminate the Chinese pagoda and the main fountain. Call to double-check prices, which vary throughout the year and often include family discounts at various times during the day. Tivoli is also open from late November to Christmas. *Vesterbrog. 3, tel. 33/15–10–01. Dkr 45. Open mid-Apr.–Sept., Mon.–Thurs. and Sun. 11 AM–midnight, Fri.–Sat. 11 AM–1 AM; late Nov.–Christmas, daily noon–9.*

TYCHO BRAHE PLANETARIUM. This modern, cylindrical planetarium, which appears to be sliced at an angle, features astronomy exhibits. The **Omnimax Theater** takes you on visual odysseys as varied as journeys through space and sea, the stages of the Rolling Stones, or Kuwaiti fires from the Persian Gulf War. These films are not recommended for children under age 7. *Gammel Kongevej 10, tel. 33/12–12–24. Dkr 75. Show times vary; open early Aug.–late June, Fri.–Mon. 10:30–9, Tues. and Thurs. 9:30–9, Wed. 9:45–9; late June–early Aug., daily 9:30–9.*

VESTERBRO. Students, union workers, and immigrants (who account for 15% of Vesterbro's population) populate this area. It's a great place to find ethnic groceries, discount shops, and cheap international restaurants. The face of Vesterbro, however, slowly has been gentrifying. Due to the city's ongoing urban-renewal and clean-up efforts, the spruced-up Vestebro is starting to attract chic cafés and eateries, along with their arty customers. The minimalist fusion restaurant–bar Delicatessen, at Vesterbrogade 120, has drawn a steady stream of Copenhageners since it joined the neighborhood. The shiny, four-star First Hotel Vesterbro is only a five-minute walk from Tivoli on Vesterbrogade. *At the southern end of Vesterbrogade.*

In This Chapter

eating out

IN COPENHAGEN, with its more than 2,000 restaurants, traditional
Danish fare spans all price categories: you can order a light lunch
of traditional smørrebrød, munch alfresco from a street-side
pølser (sausage) cart, or dine out on Limfjord oysters and local plaice.
Even the most upscale restaurants have moderate-price fixed
menus. Though few Danish restaurants require reservations, it's
best to call ahead to avoid a wait. The city's more affordable ethnic
restaurants are concentrated in Vesterbro, Nørrebro, and the side
streets off Strøget. And for less-expensive, savory noshes in stylish
surroundings, consider lingering at a café.

CATEGORY	COST*
$$$$	over Dkr 220
$$$	Dkr 160–Dkr 220
$$	Dkr 100–Dkr 160
$	under Dkr 100

*per person for a main course at dinner

RÅDHUS PLADSEN, CHRISTIANSBORG SLOT, AND STRØGET

$$$$ KONG HANS KÆLDER. Five centuries ago this was a Nordic
★ vineyard—now it's one of Scandinavia's finest restaurants. Chef
Thomas Rode Andersen's French-Danish-Asian–inspired dishes
employ the freshest local ingredients and are served in a mysterious
subterranean space with whitewashed walls and vaulted ceilings.
Try the foie gras with raspberry-vinegar sauce or the warm oysters
with salmon roe. *Vingårdstr. 6, tel. 33/11–68–68. AE, DC, MC, V. Closed
Sun. No lunch.*

copenhagen dining

Café Ketchup, 21
Copenhagen Corner, 13
Delicatessen, 7
El Meson, 5
Els, 34
Etc., 26
Flyvefisken, 11
formel B., 8
Godt, 22
Gyldne Fortun's Fiskekældere, 30

Hussmanns Vinstue, 12
Ida Davidsen, 29
Kaiseki Style, 19
Kashmir, 3
Københavner Caféen, 17
Komman-danten, 24
Kong Hans Kælder, 31
Konrad, 20
Krogs, 23

La Galette, 10
L'Alsace, 25
Le Sommelier, 33
Nyhavns Færgekro, 36
Passagens Spisehus, 9
Pasta Basta, 15
Peder Oxe, 14
Pussy Galore's Flying Circus, 2
Restaurant Le St. Jacques, 6

Riz Raz, 16
Sebastopol, 1
Skt. Gertrudes Kloster, 4
Søren K., 32
Spiseloppen, 37
Tyvenkokkenhans-koneoghende-selsker, 18
Victor, 27
Wiinblad, 28
Zeleste, 35

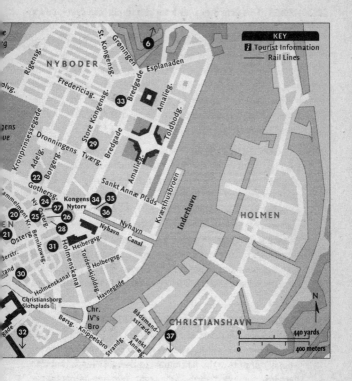

$$$$ KROGS. ★ This elegant canal-front restaurant has developed a loyal clientele—both foreign and local—for its old-fashioned atmosphere and its innovative fish dishes. Pale-green walls are simply adorned with paintings of old Copenhagen. The menu includes such specialties as pan-grilled lobster flavored with vanilla oil and monkfish fillets in a beurre-blanc sauce flavored with arugula and tomato. Jackets are recommended. *Gammel Strand 38, tel. 33/15–89–15. Reservations essential. AE, DC, MC, V. Closed Sun. and July.*

$$$$ SKT. GERTRUDES KLOSTER. The history of this medieval monastery goes back 700 years, and from the beginning its vaulted stone interiors have welcomed tradesmen and wayfarers. The dining room is bedecked with hundreds of icons, and the only light is provided by 2,000 candles. The French menu is extensive, with such specials as fresh fillet of halibut steamed in oyster sauce and l'Alsace duck breast in a sherry vinaigrette. This restaurant is sometimes too popular for its own good, and on busy weekend evenings the waitstaff can be a bit rushed. A jacket and tie are recommended. *32 Hauser Pl., tel. 33/14–66–30. Reservations essential. AE, DC, MC, V.*

$$$$ TYVENKOKKENHANSKONEOGHENDESELSKER. ★ If you've seen Peter Greenaway's dark and brilliant film *The Cook, the Thief, His Wife, and Her Lover* (with its macabre feast scenes), you may wonder what lies in store at this half-timber town-house restaurant with the same name. It's worth finding out. The same daring humor that inspired the unusual name is exhibited in the innovative seven-course menu (there is no à la carte), which changes every few weeks. You might be served baked cod in an aromatic coffee sauce or warm rooster simmered in spices and served with horseradish sauce. Desserts include pineapple with mint tortellini. Sit upstairs for a view of the cheery, orange- and yellow-walled old houses that lean against each other just across the narrow street. *Magstr. 16, tel. 33/16–12–92. Reservations essential. AE, DC, MC, V. Closed Sun. No lunch.*

$$–$$$$ GYLDNE FORTUN'S FISKEKÆLDERE. Among the city's finest seafood restaurants, this "fish cellar" is brightly decorated with seashell-shaded halogen lamps and aquariums. Across the street from Christiansborg, it is popular with politicians as well as businesspeople. Try the fillets of Scandinavian sole, which are poached in white wine, stuffed with salmon mousseline, glazed with hollandaise, and served with prawns. *Ved Stranden 18, tel. 33/ 12–20–11. Reservations essential. AE, DC, MC, V.*

$$$ SØREN K. Occupying a bright corner of the Royal Library's modern Black Diamond extension, this cool-tone restaurant, with clean lines, blond-wood furnishings, and recessed ceiling lights, serves bold French–Scandinavian concoctions using no cream, butter, or stock. The result is a menu of flavorful dishes that please the palate without weighing you down. A popular selection is the five-course menu entitled "a couple of hours in the company of fish," which has featured tuna in soy and sesame sauce or mussels drizzled with lemon and thyme. Vegetarian items include such excellent dishes as tofu marinated with red wine and topped with roasted sesame seeds, radishes, and passion fruit. For waterfront views, choose one of the many tables that sit flush up against the Black Diamond's looming glass walls. In the summer, you can enjoy your meal on the outside terrace. *Søren Kierkegaards Pl. 1 (inside the Black Diamond), tel. 45/33–47–49–49. DC, MC, V. Closed Sun.*

$–$$$ PASTA BASTA. This bright, casual eatery is always crammed with happy diners. Pasta Basta has all the ingredients for its well-deserved success: an all-you-can-eat fresh pasta and salad bar for a refreshingly low price (Dkr 69); a choice location just off the Strøget; a cheerful staff; and a decor of orange walls, an innovative mural, and glass-top tables painted in green and blue swirls. Main courses on the changing menu may include pasta with prawns, spinach, and chili peppers, or smoked salmon served with pasta in a creamy sauce of scallops, spinach, and herbs. Pasta Basta is one of the city's only restaurants (barring fast-food and shawarma joints) that serves food until 3 AM (and until 5 AM on Friday and Saturday). During these early morning hours, the restaurant is popular with dancers and musicians from the Royal Theater and other venues, who come in to relax and dine after their evening performances. *Valkendorfsg. 22, tel. 33/11–21–31. DC, MC, V.*

$$ COPENHAGEN CORNER. Diners here are treated to a superb view of the Rådhus Pladsen, as well as to terrific smørrebrød, both of which compensate for the uneven pace of the often-harried but hard-working staff and some of the food. Specialties include fried veal with bouillon gravy and fried potatoes; entrecôte in garlic and bordelaise sauce paired with creamed potatoes; and a herring plate with three types of spiced, marinated herring and boiled potatoes. *H. C. Andersens Blvd. 1A, tel. 33/91–45–45. AE, DC, MC, V.*

$$ EL MESON. At this Spanish restaurant, you are seated at smoothly worn wooden tables in a dimly lit dining room decorated with earthen crockery. The knowledgeable waitstaff serves generous portions of beef spiced with spearmint, lamb with honey sauce, and paella Valenciano—a mixture of rice, chicken, ham, shrimp, lobster, squid, green beans, and peas—for two. *Hauser Pl. 12 (behind Kultorvet), tel. 33/11–91–31. DC, MC, V. Closed Sun. No lunch.*

$$ FLYVEFISKEN. Silvery stenciled fish swim along blue-and-yellow walls in this Thai eatery. Spicy concoctions include chicken with cashew nuts and herring shark in basil sauce. The less-expensive health-food café Atlas Bar—in the basement—serves excellent food to a steady stream of students and hipsters. *Lars Bjørnstr. 18, tel. 33/14–95–15. DC, MC, V. Closed Sun. No lunch (Atlas Bar open lunch and dinner).*

$$ HUSSMANNS VINSTUE. Founded in 1888, this warmly lit basement restaurant is housed in a former stable dating from 1727, which accounts for the low ceilings. If you're looking for old-world Denmark, this is it. Beer mugs dangle above the bar, dark-green lamps shed light onto the heavy wooden tables, and black-and-white photographs of Copenhagen hang on the walls. Until 1981, women were allowed to enter only if accompanied by a male, a rule that was established by one of the restaurant's female owners. For more than 100 years, Hussmans has proudly served hearty

Danish smørrebrød to everyone from Walt Disney to the Danish royal family. While other Danish lunch spots may serve salads and lighter cuisine, at Hussmans Vinstue you can feast on all types of herring (fried, curried, marinated, and spiced), smoked eel with scrambled eggs, beef tartare with egg yolk, homemade sausage, and roast beef with potato salad, all served on your choice of rye or white bread. *Larsbjørnsstræde 2, tel. 33/11–58–86. Reservations essential. MC, V.*

$$ KAISEKI STYLE. Near the Strøget, this serene sushi restaurant with blond-wood furnishings and spare Japanese table settings provides a welcome respite from the walking street crowds. Young owner Sigurd Pieter Bruin, a long-time sushi lover and frequent visitor to Japan, is particularly proud of the small sushi bar (there are only about five seats), where diners can watch and, more important, communicate with the sushi chef while he's preparing their order. The fresh and flavorful sushi includes shrimp, tuna, white fish, and salmon. The nicely priced bento box lunches start at Dkr 78 and include shrimp dumplings, California rolls, a potato croquette, salad, and rice. The restaurant has a selection of top-notch sake. *Rådhusstr. 4, tel. 33/91–50–60. MC, V.*

$$ PEDER OXE. On a 17th-century square, this lively, countrified bistro has rustic tables and 15th-century Portuguese tiles. All entrées—among them grilled steaks and fish and the best fancy burgers in town—come with an excellent self-service salad bar. Damask-covered tables are set with heavy cutlery and opened bottles of hearty Pyrénées wine. A clever call-light for the waitress is above each table. In spring, when the high northern sun is shining but the warmth still has not kicked in, you won't do badly sitting outside in the Gråbrødretorv (Gray Friars' Square) sipping drinks while wrapped in blankets left thoughtfully for patrons in wicker chairs. *Gråbrødretorv 11, tel. 33/11–00–77. DC, MC, V.*

$–$$ KØBENHAVNER CAFÉEN. You know you're in for a real Danish meal when you can smell the vinegary rød kål (red cabbage, a Danish staple) upon entering. Dimly lit and warm, with a dark wood and burgundy decor, this local's favorite just oozes with hyggelig. Old photographs of Danish royalty line the walls, and a 1798 street lamp stands alongside the inviting bar. Choose from a wide range of smørrebrød selections and also a formidable lineup of down-home Danish dishes such as *frikkedeller* (pork meatballs) and butter-fried salmon with boiled potatoes. In the summer the kitchen offers a traditional Danish Christmas meal "so that everyone can experience Denmark's Christmas traditions." The meal includes roast pork with red cabbage and the much-loved *ris à l'amande* (rice pudding) for dessert. Hidden inside is an almond, and whoever finds it receives a small present. These summer Christmas meals have become so popular that they are generally offered only to tour groups, but it's worth asking when you reserve. *Badstuestr. 10, tel. 33/32–80–81. Reservations essential weekends. MC, V.*

$–$$ RIZ RAZ. On a corner off Strøget, this Middle Eastern restaurant hops with young locals, families, couples, and anyone who appreciates good value and spicy fare. The inexpensive all-you-can-eat buffet is heaped with lentils, tomatoes, potatoes, olives, hummus, warm pita bread, yogurt and cucumbers, pickled vegetables, and bean salads. Don't be put off by the hordes—just join them, either in the restaurant's endless labyrinth of dining rooms or in the jam-packed summertime patio. *Kompagnistr. 20, tel. 33/15–05–75. Reservations essential weekends. DC, MC, V.*

$ LA GALETTE. Tucked into a bright little courtyard, this cheery creperie serves an array of delectable crepes, including the Asterix crepe, stuffed with ratatouille, egg, and chives, and the Quimper, with spinach, egg, bacon, and cheese. The luscious lineup of sweet crepes includes everything from banana and chocolate to flambéed caramel apples. *Larbjørnsstr. 9, tel. 33/32–37–90. MC, V. No lunch Sun.*

AROUND AMALIENBORG AND NORTH

$$$$ ETC. Copenhagen's beautiful people meet languid Morocco in this über-hip North African–influenced restaurant. The black-turtleneck brigade and models of both sexes lounge on very low oversize couches with zebra-print throw pillows and sip exorbitantly priced cocktails. The dinner menu includes pricey but superb set menus of fresh fish and meat platters, and main courses such as fried Norwegian salmon flavored with Caribbean fruit juice and mint. A DJ starts spinning tunes around midnight on Friday and Saturday, when Etc. stays open until 4 AM; the rest of the week it closes at midnight. *Hovedvagtsg. 8, tel. 33/33–99–97. AE, DC, MC, V. Closed Sun.–Mon. No lunch.*

$$$$ GODT. The name says it all: this elegant little two-story restaurant with cool gray walls, silvery curtain partitions, and tulips in clear-glass bottles is *godt* (good). Actually, it's very, very good—so good that Godt has become the buzz of the town. The superb French–Danish menu showcases Chef Colin Rice's commitment to fresh ingredients and seasonal produce, which he buys every morning. Rice prepares a set daily menu, and you can choose to have three, four, or five courses. Dishes may include a black-bean and crab soup or a fillet of venison drizzled with truffle sauce. *Gothersg. 38, tel. 33/15–21–22. Reservations essential. DC, MC, V. Closed Sun.–Mon. No lunch.*

$$$$ KOMMANDANTEN. Fancifully decorated by master florist Tage ★ Andersen with brushed iron and copper furniture, down pillows, and foliage-flanked lights, this is among the city's most exclusive dinner spots, attracting well-heeled businesspeople and local celebrities. The adventuresome international fare might include dishes such as rabbit with bouillon-cooked lentils, herbs, and bacon, and marinated salmon with oysters and parsley. Jackets are recommended. *Ny Adelg. 7, tel. 33/12–09–90. AE, DC, MC, V. Closed Sun. No lunch Sat.*

$$$–$$$$ ELS. When it opened in 1853, the intimate Els was the place to be seen before the theater, and the painted Muses on the walls still watch diners rush to make an eight o'clock curtain. Antique wooden columns complement the period furniture, including tables inlaid with Royal Copenhagen tile work. The nouvelle French four-course menu changes every two weeks, always incorporating game, fish, and market produce. Jackets are recommended. *Store Strandestr. 3, tel. 33/14–13–41. AE, DC, MC, V. Closed July. No lunch Sun.*

$–$$$$ CAFÉ KETCHUP. You have a choice at this informal, upbeat eatery: for light meals (at light prices), try the lively front café, where you can settle into a red-and-white wicker chair next to the large picture windows and watch the world go by on chic Pilestræde. Try the spring rolls with smoked salmon and cod, flavored with ginger and coriander. It also serves a tasty brunch (yogurt with muesli, toast with turkey, mozzarella, and bacon, and black currant–fig marmalade) from 10–1. For more-substantial fare, venture into the restaurant decorated with old French Perrier ads and lit with white candles. Starters include a potato–wasabi soup served with a spicy crab cake, and bruschetta topped with a mango salsa. Main dishes range from halibut stuffed with crabmeat and herbs to marinated duck breast served with sun-dried tomatoes and fennel salad sprinkled with pine nuts. By night, the place turns into a lively bar and club. There is also a Café Ketchup in Tivoli, with a large terrace and a similar menu. *Pilestr. 19, tel. 33/ 32–30–30. DC, MC, V. Closed Sun.*

$$$ KONRAD. ★ Elegant and minimalist, this restaurant attracts young people and stars, many of whom look like they just walked off a fashion runway. Considering its linear, beige decor, the restaurant seems as geared for people-watching as dining. The French–international menu is inventive without being off-the-wall, with offerings such as potato tortellini filled with oysters and white cream sauce. *Pilestr. 12–14, tel. 33/93–29–29. Reservations essential. AE, DC, MC, V. Closed Sun.*

$$$ L'ALSACE. ★ Set in the cobbled courtyard off Pistolstræde and hung with paintings by Danish surrealist Wilhelm Freddie, this restaurant is peaceful and quiet, and has attracted such diverse diners as Queen Margrethe, Elton John, and Pope John Paul II. The hand-drawn menu lists oysters from Brittany, terrine de foie gras, and *choucrôute à la Strasbourgeoise* (a hearty mélange of cold cabbage, homemade sausage, and pork). Try the superb fresh-fruit tarts and cakes for dessert, and ask to sit in the patio overlooking the courtyard. *Ny Østerg. 9, tel. 33/14–57–43. AE, DC, MC, V. Closed Sun.*

$$$ LE SOMMELIER. ★ The grande dame of Copenhagen's French restaurants is appropriately named. The cellar boasts more than 800 varieties of wine, and you can order many of them by the glass. Exquisite French dishes are complemented by an elegant interior of pale yellow walls, rough-hewn wooden floors, brass chandeliers, and hanging copper pots. Dishes include guinea fowl in a foie gras sauce or lamb shank and crispy sweetbreads with parsley and garlic. While waiting for your table, you can sidle up to the burnished dark-wood and brass bar and begin sampling the wine. *Bredg. 63–65, tel. 33/12–09–90. Reservations essential. DC, MC, V. No lunch weekends.*

$$$ WIINBLAD. This restaurant in the D'Angleterre hotel doubles as a gallery inspired by the work of contemporary Danish artist Bjørn Wiinblad. Almost everything—tiles, wall partitions, plaques, candlesticks, vases, and even some tables—has been made by the great Dane, and the effect is bright, cheerful, and very elegant. The eatery offers an ample breakfast buffet, lunch, a fabulous and surprisingly affordable tea, and grilled specialties for dinner. Try the pickled herring with new potatoes that's topped with sour cream, or the breast of duck in cranberry cream sauce. *D'Angleterre, Kongens Nytorv 34, tel. 33/12–80–95. AE, DC, MC, V.*

$$ IDA DAVIDSEN. Five generations old, this world-renowned lunch spot is synonymous with smørrebrød. Dimly lit, with worn wooden tables and news clippings of famous visitors, it's usually packed. Creative sandwiches include the H. C. Andersen, with liver pâté, bacon, and tomatoes. The terrific smoked duck is smoked by Ida's husband, Adam, and served alongside a horseradish-spiked cabbage salad. *Store Kongensg. 70, tel. 33/91–36–55. Reservations essential. DC, MC, V. Closed weekends and July. No dinner.*

$$ RESTAURANT LE ST. JACQUES. ★ This tiny restaurant barely accommodates a dozen tables, but whenever the sun shines, diners spill out of its icon-filled dining room to sit at tables facing busy Østerbrogade. The chef and owners come from some of the finest restaurants in town, but claim they started this place to slow down the pace and enjoy the company of their customers. The fare changes according to what is available at the market, but expect fabulous concoctions—smoked salmon with crushed eggplant, Canadian scallops with leeks and salmon roe in a beurre blanc sauce, sole with basil sauce and reduced balsamic glaze, and a savory *poussin* (young, small chicken) with sweetbreads scooped into phyllo pastry atop a bed of polenta and lentils. Close tables and chitchat with the owners give this a true café atmosphere. *Skt. Jacobs Pl. 1, tel. 35/42–77–07. Reservations essential. DC, MC, V.*

$$ VICTOR. Excellent people-watching and good bistro fare are the calling cards at this French-style corner café. It's best during weekend lunches, when young and old gather for such specialties as rib roast, homemade pâté, and smoked salmon and cheese platters. Come here for one of the best brunches in town. Be warned however that the formal restaurant in the back of the space is quite expensive—order from the front café side for a less expensive meal. *Ny Østerg. 8, tel. 33/13–36–13. AE, DC, MC, V. No dinner Sun.*

$$ ZELESTE. Outfitted with a short but well-worn bar, a covered and heated atrium, and—upstairs—a U-shape dining room, Zeleste serves as a soothing respite to Nyhavn's canal-front party. Although the food is usually excellent, if you're ravenous, ask specifically about portions—otherwise, you could end up with some tiny slivers of fried fois gras or a few tortellini. For lunch, the famished will do well with either the focaccia sandwich or the lobster salad served with toast and an excellent roux dressing; if the salad is not at your table within five minutes, you get a free glass of champagne. *Store Strandstr. 6, tel. 33/16–06–06. DC, MC, V.*

$ **NYHAVNS FÆRGEKRO.** Locals pack into this waterfront café every day at lunchtime, when the staff unveils a buffet with 10 kinds of herring. An unsavory sailor's bar when Nyhavn was the city's port, the butter-yellow building retains a rustic charm. Waiters duck under rough wood beams when they deliver your choice of the delicious dinner specials, which might be salmon with dill sauce or steak with shaved truffles. In summer, sit outside and order an aquavit, the local liqueur that tastes like caraway seeds. *Nyhavn 5, tel. 33/15–15–88. DC, MC, V.*

DOWN NØRREBRO

$$$$ **FORMEL B.** The name stands for "basic formula," but this French–Danish fusion restaurant, with chef Nicolaj Kirk at the helm, is anything but basic. Kirk, a third-generation chef, is fanatical about freshness, and this comes through in every dish. Dishes might include mussel soup flavored with wood sorrel; smoked salmon with dill seeds, spinach, and bacon; or panfried chicken with parsley root and horseradish, accompanied by all its parts— the liver, the heart, the craw, and the red comb—served on an array of small plates. The dessert plate is a work of art: a collection of individual delicacies are arranged on a large white eye-shape platter, and drizzled with a passion fruit glaze and pine nuts. Kirk prepares a seven-course menu (Dkr 495) daily, depending on what seasonal ingredients are available. There is no à la carte menu. *Vesterbrog. 182, tel. 35/37–54–71. AE, MC, V. Closed Sun. No lunch.*

$$–$$$$ **PASSAGENS SPISEHUS.** Tucked into a *passagens* (passageway) just steps from the Det Ny Teater (New Theater), this restaurant is leading the rediscovery of Scandinavia's culinary roots. Starters include smoked heart of reindeer, thinly sliced, served on a bed of marinated onions and beans, and a cream soup with potatoes, carrots, dill, and Baltic salmon. For your main dish, you can carve into bear from the Swedish woods with stuffed cabbage, potatoes,

and sweetened beets or fillet of Lapland reindeer with seasonal vegetables. The elegant interior has dark-wood walls, black leather chairs, and soft white globes of light hanging over every table. It's popular with theater-goers who come for the fixed-price theater menu, which includes two or three courses and changes daily. *Vesterbrog. 42, tel. 33/22–47–87. MC, V. No lunch.*

$$ DELICATESSEN. Happily defying labels, this casual diner–café–bar is done in Dansk design—silver-gray bucket seats and a stainless steel-top bar—and serves hearty brunches and global cuisine by day, and cocktails and DJ-spun dance tunes by night. Linger over scrambled eggs with bacon and a steaming cup of coffee (served from 11 AM), or tuck into the international cuisine of the month, which runs from North African to Thai to Italian. The menu might include pad thai; lamb curry with basmati rice, mint, and yogurt; or roast pork with thyme and zucchini. A trip to the bathroom is good for grins: On your way you pass by two fun-house mirrors; look to one side, and you're squat and fat. Look to the other, and you're slender and tall. *Vesterbrog. 120, tel. 33/22–16–33. V.*

IN AND AROUND VESTERBROGADE

$–$$ PUSSY GALORE'S FLYING CIRCUS. Done up with a few Arne Jacobsen swan chairs, naive wall paintings, and tables smashed up against each other, this trendy gathering place is supposed to be as kitsch as its name. Although the mix of decor is retro and does a good job of setting a '60s stage, the regulars who come here make it feel more like a low-key neighborhood bar. Frequented by both young families and black-clad poseurs, this place serves surprisingly down-to-earth and affordable fare, with eggs and bacon and other brunch items along with hefty burgers and wok-fried delectables. *Skt. Hans Torv, tel. 35/24–53–00. DC, MC, V.*

$–$$ SEBASTOPOL. Students and locals crowd this laid-back eatery for brunch and on weekend evenings, but it's a good choice if you want to get off the beaten tourist path. The menu is varied with lots of salads, warm sandwiches, and burgers—and just about the most American–style brunch in the city. When it's warm, tables are set outside on the square, where there's great people-watching. *Skt. Hans Torv, tel. 35/36–30–02. Reservations not accepted. MC, V.*

$ KASHMIR. The quiet, carpet-shrouded Indian restaurant is a favorite with locals, who come for the unusual vegetarian and fish menu. Specialties include tandoori-fried salmon, a hearty lentil soup, and the basic side dishes—such as *bhajis* (fried vegetables patties); *raita* (yogurt and cucumbers); and naan, Indian flat bread cooked in the tandoori oven. *Nørrebrog. 35, tel. 35/37–54–71. DC, MC, V.*

CHRISTIANIA

$$–$$$ SPISELOPPEN. Round out your visit to the Free State of Christiania with a meal at Spiseloppen, a 160-seat warehouse restaurant that was a military storage facility and an army canteen in its former life. Upon entering Christiania, wind your way past shaggy dogs, their shaggy owners, graffiti murals, and wafts of patchouli. (There are few street signs, so just ask; Spisseloppen is the neighborhood's best-known restaurant.) From the outside, this run-down warehouse with splintered windows may seem a bit foreboding, but inside it's a different story. Climb up rickety stairs to the second floor and you're rewarded with a loft-size dining room with low, wood-beamed ceilings and candles flickering on the tables. The menu highlights are fresh and inventive vegetarian and fish dishes, which might include artichokes stuffed with eggplant and Portobello mushrooms, served with squash, mango, and papaya. One floor down is Loppen, a club that hosts mid-week jazz sessions, and DJ dance nights on the weekends. *Bådmandsstr. 43, tel. 32/57–95–58. MC, V. Closed Mon. No lunch.*

In This Chapter

shopping

A SHOWCASE FOR WORLD-FAMOUS DANISH DESIGN and craftsmanship, Copenhagen seems to have been designed with shoppers in mind. The best buys are such luxury items as crystal, porcelain, silver, and furs. Look for offers and sales (*tilbud* or *udsalg* in Danish) and check antiques and secondhand shops for classics at cut-rate prices.

Although prices are inflated by a hefty 25% Value-Added Tax (Danes call it MOMS), non–European Union citizens can receive about an 18% refund. For more details and a list of all tax-free shops, ask at the tourist board for a copy of the *Tax-Free Shopping Guide*.

The **CRAFTS.DK INFORMATION CENTER FOR DANISH CRAFTS AND DESIGN** (Amagertorv 1, tel. 33/12–61–62, www.craftsdk. com) provides helpful information (including a map) on the city's galleries, shops, and workshops specializing in Danish crafts and design, from jewelry to ceramics to wooden toys to furniture. Its Web site has listings and reviews of the city's best crafts shops.

DEPARTMENT STORES

HENNES & MAURITZ (Amagertorv 11, tel. 33/32–60–09), H & M for short, has stores all over town. They offer reasonably priced clothing and accessories for men, women, and children; best of all are the to-die-for baby clothes. **ILLUM** (Østerg. 52, tel. 33/14–40–02), not to be confused with Illums Bolighus, is well stocked, with a lovely rooftop café and excellent basement grocery.

MAGASIN (Kongens Nytorv 13, tel. 33/11–44–33), Scandinavia's largest, also has a top-quality basement marketplace.

SHOPPING DISTRICTS, STREETS, AND MALLS

The pedestrian-only **STRØGET** and adjacent Købmagergade are the shopping streets, but wander down the smaller streets for lower-priced, offbeat stores. The most exclusive shops are at the end of Strøget, around Kongens Nytorv, and on Ny Adelgade, Grønnegade, and Pistolstræde. **KRONPRINSENSGADE** has become the in-vogue fashion strip, where a number of young Danish clothing designers have opened boutiques. **BREDGADE**, just off Kongens Nytorv, is lined with elegant antique and silver shops, furniture stores, and auction houses. **SCALA**, a city-center mall across the street from Tivoli, has several clothing stores, a couple of boisterous pubs, and a main-floor food court for the famished. Copenhagen's latest mall is the gleaming **FISKETORVET SHOPPING CENTER**, built in what was Copenhagen's old fish market. It's near the canal, south of the city center, within walking distance to the Dybbølsbro station. It includes all the usual mall shops, from chain clothing stores (Mango, Hennes & Mauritz); shoe shops (including the ubiquitous Ecco) to a smattering of jewelry, watch, and stereo retailers, such as Swatch and Bang & Olufsen. Fast-food outlets abound. In the south part of the city, on **VESTERBROGADE,** you can find discount stores—especially leather and clothing shops.

SPECIALTY STORES

Antiques

For silver, porcelain, and crystal, the well-stocked shops on **BREDGADE** are upscale and expensive. Spacious and elegant, **DANSK MØBELKUNST** (Bredg. 32, tel. 33/32–38–37) is home to one of the city's largest collections of vintage Danish furniture, including pieces by Arne Jacobsen, Kaare Klimt, and Finn Juhl, whose lustrous, rosewood furnishings are among some of the finest examples of Danish design.

DANBORG GOLD AND SILVER (Holbergsg. 17, tel. 33/32–93–94) is one of the best places for estate jewelry and silver flatware. For silver, Christmas plates, or porcelain, head to **H. DANIELSENS** (Læderstr. 11, tel. 33/13–02–74). **KAABERS ANTIKVARIAT** (Skinderg. 34, tel. 33/15–41–77) is an emporium for old and rare books, prints, and maps. The dozens of **RAVNSBORGGADE** stores carry traditional pine, oak, and mahogany furniture, and smaller items such as lamps and tableware. Some of them sell tax-free items and can arrange shipping. On Strøget, **ROYAL COPENHAGEN** (Amagertorv 6, tel. 33/13–71–81) carries old and new china, porcelain patterns, and figurines, as well as seconds.

Audio Equipment

For high-tech design and acoustics, **BANG & OLUFSEN** (Østerg. 3, tel. 33/15–04–22) is so renowned that its products are in the permanent design collection of New York's Museum of Modern Art. (Check prices at home first to make sure you are getting a deal.) You can find B&O and other international names at **FREDGAARD** (Nørre Voldg. 17, tel. 33/13–82–45), near Nørreport Station.

Clothing

It used to be that Danish clothing design took a back seat to the famous Dansk-designed furniture and silver, but increasingly that's no longer the case. If you're on the prowl for the newest Danish designs, you'll find a burgeoning number of cooperatives and designer-owned stores around town, particularly along Kronprinsensgade, near the Strøget.

ARTIUM (Vesterbrog. 1, tel. 33/12–34–88) offers an array of colorful, Scandinavian-designed sweaters and clothes alongside useful and artful household gifts. Every stylish Dane probably has at least one item from **BRUUNS BAZAAR** (Kronprinsensg. 8–9, tel. 33/32–19–99) hanging in the closet. Here you can buy the Bruuns label—inspired designs with a classic, clean-cut Danish look—and other high-end names, including Gucci. The **COMPANY STORE** (Frederiksbergg. 24, tel. 33/11–35–55) is for trendy, youthful styles, typified by the Danish Matinique label. Among the most inventive handmade women's clothing shops is **MET MARI** (Vesterg. 11, tel. 33/15–87–25). **MUNTHE PLUS SIMONSEN** (Kronprinsensg. 8, tel. 33/32–03–12 women's wear; 33/32–89–12 men's wear) sells innovative and playful—and pricey—Danish designs. **PETITGAS CHAPEAUX** (Købmagerg. 5, tel. 33/13–62–70) is a venerable shop for old-fashioned men's hats. Thick, traditional, patterned, and solid Scandinavian sweaters are available at the **SWEATER MARKET** (Frederiksbergg. 15, tel. 33/15–27–73).

Crystal and Porcelain

Minus the V.A.T., such Danish classics as Holmegaards crystal and Royal Copenhagen porcelain usually are less expensive than they are back home. Signed art glass is always more expensive, but be on the lookout for seconds as well as secondhand and unsigned pieces. **ROSENTHAL STUDIO-HAUS** (Frederiksberg. 21, on Strøget, tel. 33/14–21–02) offers the lead-crystal wildlife reliefs of Mats Johansson as well as the very modern functional and decorative works of many other Italian and Scandinavian artisans. **BODUM HUS** (Østerg. 10, on Strøget, tel. 33/36–40–80) shows off a wide variety of reasonably priced Danish-designed functional, and especially kitchen-oriented, accoutrements; the milk foamers are indispensable for cappuccino lovers. **SKANDINAVISK GLAS** (Ny Østerg. 4, tel. 33/13–80–95) has a large selection of Danish and international glass and a helpful, informative staff.

The **ROYAL COPENHAGEN** shop (Amagertorv 6, tel. 33/13–71–81) has firsts and seconds. For a look at the goods at their source, try the **ROYAL COPENHAGEN FACTORY** (Smalleg. 45, tel. 38/14–48–48). Holmegaards Glass can be purchased at either the Royal Copenhagen store on Amagertorv or at the factory on Smallegade (for seconds); alternatively, you can travel to their dedicated factory (tel. 55/54–50–00), 97 km (60 mi) south of Copenhagen near the town of Næstved.

Design

GUBI DESIGN (Grønnegade 10, tel. 33/32–63–68) is where to go for the super-clean *Wallpaper* look. The chic kitchens are amazing and amazingly priced, but if you can't afford to move one back home, you can at least gain inspiration before you remodel your own kitchen. Part gallery, part department store, **ILLUMS BOLIGHUS** (Amagertorv 6, tel. 33/14–19–41) shows off cutting-edge Danish and international design—art glass, porcelain, silverware, carpets, and loads of grown-up toys. **LYSBERG, HANSEN AND THERP** (Bredg. 75, tel. 33/14–47–87), one of the most prestigious interior-design firms in Denmark, has sumptuous showrooms done up in traditional and modern styles. At **PAUSTIAN** (Paustian Kalkbrænderiløbskaj 2, tel. 39/16–65–65), you can peruse elegant contemporary furniture and accessories in a building designed by Dane Jørn Utzon, the architect of the Sydney Opera House. You can also have a gourmet lunch at the Restaurant Paustian. (It's open only for lunch.) Wizard florist **TAGE ANDERSEN** (Ny Adelg. 12, tel. 33/93–09–13) has a fantasy-infused gallery–shop filled with one-of-a-kind gifts and arrangements; browsers (who generally don't purchase the expensive items) are charged a Dkr 40 admission.

Fur

Denmark, the world's biggest producer of ranched minks, is the place to go for quality furs. Furs are ranked into four grades: Saga Royal (the best), Saga, Quality 1, and Quality 2. Copenhagen's finest furrier, dealing only in Saga Royal quality, and purveyor to the royal family is **BIRGER CHRISTENSEN** (Østerg. 38, tel. 33/11–55–55), which presents a new collection yearly from its in-house design team. Expect to spend about 20% less than in the United States for same-quality furs ($5,000–$10,000 for mink, $3,000 for a fur-lined coat) but as in all things related to finding a deal, do your homework before you leave home. Birger Christensen is also among the preeminent fashion houses in town, carrying Donna Karan, Chanel, Prada, Kenzo, Jil Sander, and Yves Saint Laurent. **A. C. BANG** (Vesterbrogade 1, tel. 33/15–17–26), close to Tivoli, carries less expensive furs than Birger Christensen, but has an old-world, old-money aura and very high quality.

Silver

Check the silver standard of a piece by its stamp. Three towers and "925S" (which means 925 parts out of 1,000) mark sterling. Two towers are used for silver plate. The "826S" stamp (also denoting sterling, but less pure) was used until the 1920s. Even with shipping charges, you can expect to save 50% versus American prices when buying Danish silver (especially used) at the source. For one of the most recognized names in international silver, visit **GEORG JENSEN** (Amagertorv 4, tel. 33/11–40–80), an elegant, austere shop aglitter with sterling. Jensen has its own museum next door. Owned by long-time Jensen collector Gregory Pepin, **DANISH SILVER** (Bredg. 22, tel. 33/11–52–52) houses a remarkable collection of classic Jensen designs, from hollowware and place settings to Art Deco jewelry. Pepin, an American who has lived in Denmark for over a decade, is a font of information on Danish silver design, so if you're in the market, it's well worth stopping by. According to Pepin, the first time that the earliest Jensen designs can officially be called antiques will be in 2004, 100 years after Jensen first created them.

ERA HARTOGSOHN (Palæg. 8, tel. 33/15–53–98) carries all sorts of silver knickknacks and settings. The **ENGLISH SILVER HOUSE**

(Pilestr. 4, tel. 33/14–83–81) is an emporium of used estate silver. **PETER KROG** (4 Bredg., tel. 33/12–45–55) stocks collectors' items in silver, primarily Georg Jensen place settings, compotes, and jewelry. The city's largest (and brightest) silver store is **SØLVKÆLDEREN** (Kompagnistr. 1, tel. 33/13–36–34), with an endless selection of tea services, place settings, and jewelry.

STREET MARKETS

Check with the tourist board or the tourist magazine *Copenhagen This Week* for flea markets. Bargaining is expected. The junk and flea market that takes place Saturday in summer and stretches from Nørrebros Runddel down the road along the Assistens Kirkegaard (cemetery) claims to be one of the longest in the world. For a good overview of antiques and junk, visit the flea market at **ISRAELS PLADS** (near Nørreport Station), open May through October, Saturday 8–2. It is run by more than 100 professional dealers, and prices are steep, but there are loads of classic Danish porcelain, silver, jewelry, and crystal, plus books, prints, postcards, and more. Slightly smaller than the Israels Plads market, and with lower prices and more junk, is the market behind **FREDERIKSBERG RÅDHUS** (open summer Saturday mornings).

In This Chapter

outdoor activities and sports

GET OUTSIDE AND GET MOVING with the huge variety of sports and recreational facilities that Copenhagen has to offer. Renting a bicycle is a great way to keep fit and explore this bike-friendly city. Soccer is an immensely popular sport in Denmark; catch a game at the Parken stadium. Or you can get away from the bustle of the city at one of the many beaches around Copenhagen.

PARTICIPANT AND SPECTATOR SPORTS

Beaches

North of Copenhagen along the old beach road, **STRANDVEJEN,** is a string of lovely old seaside towns and beaches. **BELLEVUE BEACH** (across the street from Klampenborg Station) is packed with locals and has cafés, kiosks, and surfboard rentals. **CHARLOTTENLUND FORT** (Bus 6 from Rådhus Pl.) is a bit more private, but you have to pay (about Dkr 20) to swim off the pier. The beaches along the tony town of **VEDBÆK**, 18 km (11 mi) north of Copenhagen, are not very crowded as they are not as close to Copenhagen nor as easily accessible by public transportation.

Biking

Bike rentals (Dkr 100–Dkr 300 deposit and Dkr 35–Dkr 70 per day) are available throughout the city, and most roads have bike lanes. You might also be lucky and find an advertisement-flanked "city bike," parked at busy points around the city including Kongens Nytorv and the Nørreport train station. Deposit Dkr 20 and pedal away; your money is returned when you return the bike. The city bikes are available from May to September. The tourist office has city bike maps with suggested bike routes including a route of the city's ramparts or of the Copenhagen harbor. Follow all traffic signs and signals; bicycle lights and reflectors must be used at night. The **DANISH CYCLIST FEDERATION** (Rømersg. 7, tel. 33/32–31–21) has information about biking in the city.

Golf

Some clubs do not accept reservations; call for details. Virtually all clubs in Denmark require you to be a member of some other golf club for admittance. Handicap requirements vary widely.

The 18-hole **KØBENHAVNS GOLF KLUB** (Dyrehaven 2, tel. 39/63–04–83) is said to be Scandinavia's oldest. Greens fees range from Dkr 180 to Dkr 240. One of Denmark's best courses, often the host of international tournaments, is the 18-hole **RUNGSTED GOLF KLUB** (Vestre Stationsvej 16, tel. 45/86–34–44). A 30 handicap for all players is required on weekdays; on weekends and holidays there's a 24 handicap for men and a 29 handicap for women.

Health and Fitness Clubs

A day pass for weights and aerobics at the **FITNESS CLUB** (Vesterbrog. 2E at Scala, across the street from Tivoli, tel. 33/32–10–02) is Dkr 75. **FORM OG FITNESS** (Form and Fitness) offers one-day aerobics passes for Dkr 75 at the SAS Globetrotter Hotel (Engvej 171, tel. 32/55–00–70) in Amager, and a pool, weights, treadmill, and stationary bikes for Dkr 75 at the SAS Scandinavia Hotel (Amager Boulevarden 70, tel. 32/54–28–88), and weights, aerobics, and stationary bikes in Østerbro (Øster Allé 42, tel. 35/55-00-71).

Horseback Riding

You can ride at the Dyrehavebakken (Deer Forest Hills) at the **FORTUNENS PONYUDLEJNING** (Ved Fortunen 33, Lyngby, tel. 45/87-60-58). A one-hour session (English saddle), in which both experienced and inexperienced riders go out with a guide, costs about Dkr 95.

Running

The 6-km (4-mi) loop around the three lakes just west of city center—Skt. Jørgens, Peblinge, and Sortedams—is a runner's nirvana. There are also paths at the Rosenborg Have; the Frederiksberg Garden (near Frederiksberg Station, corner of Frederiksberg Allé and Pile Allé); and the Dyrehaven, north of the city near Klampenborg.

Soccer

Danish soccer fans call themselves Rolegans, which loosely translates as well-behaved fans as opposed to hooligans. These Rolegans idolize the national team's soccer players as superstars. When the rivalry is most intense (especially against Sweden and Norway), fans don face paint, wear head-to-toe red and white, incessantly wave the Dannebrog (Danish flag), and have a good time whether or not they win. The biggest stadium in town for national and international games is **PARKEN** (Øster Allé 50, tel. 35/43-31-31). Tickets (Dkr 140 for slightly obstructed views, Dkr 220–Dkr 320 for unobstructed; local matches are less expensive than international ones) can be bought through Billetnet (tel. 38/88-70-22).

Swimming

Swimming is very popular here, and the pools (all of which are indoor) are crowded but well maintained. Separate bath tickets can also be purchased. Admission to local pools (Dkr 20–Dkr 50) includes a locker key, but you have to bring your own towel. Most pools are 25 meters long. The **DGI BYEN SWIM CENTER** (Tietgensg. 65, tel. 33/29–80–00) is metropolitan Copenhagen's newest addition, with a massive oval pool with 100-meter lanes and a nifty platform in the middle that can be raised for parties and conferences. The swim center also has a children's pool and a "mountain pool," with a climbing wall, wet trampoline, and several diving boards. Admission to the swim center is Dkr 46. Once a month, it hosts popular "spa nights" (Dkr 249), when candles are placed around the pool, dinner and wine is served on the raised pool platform, and massages and other spa services are offered. The beautiful **FREDERIKSBERG SVØMMEHAL** (Helgesvej 29, tel. 38/14–04–04) maintains its old art-deco decor of sculptures and decorative tiles. The 50-meter **LYNGBY SVØMMEHAL** (Lundoftevej 53, tel. 45/87–44–56) has a separate diving pool. In the modern concrete **VESTERBRO SVØMMEHAL** (Angelg. 4, tel. 33/22–05–00), many enjoy swimming next to the large glass windows.

Tennis

Courts fees for guests are very high, often including court rental (around Dkr 85 per person) and a separate nonmembers' user fee (as high as Dkr 140). If you must volley, courts are available to guests at some sports centers before 1 PM only. **HELLERUP IDRÆTS KLUB** (Hartmannsvej 37, tel. 39/62–14–28) is about 5 km (3 mi) north of town. **KØBENHAVNS BOLDKLUB** (PeterBangs Vej 147, tel. 38/71–41–50) is in Frederiksberg, a neighborhood just west of central Copenhagen. **SKOVSHOVED IDRÆTS FORENING** (Krørsvej 5A, tel. 39/64–23–83) is along the old beach road about 10 km (6 mi) north of town.

Distance Conversion Chart

Kilometers/Miles

To change kilometers (km) to miles (mi), multiply km by .621.
To change mi to km, multiply mi by 1.61.

km to mi	mi to km
1 = .62	1 = 1.6
2 = 1.2	2 = 3.2
3 = 1.9	3 = 4.8
4 = 2.5	4 = 6.4
5 = 3.1	5 = 8.1
6 = 3.7	6 = 9.7
7 = 4.3	7 = 11.3
8 = 5.0	8 = 12.9

Meters/Feet

To change meters (m) to feet (ft), multiply m by 3.28.
To change ft to m, multiply ft by .305.

m to ft	ft to m
1 = 3.3	1 = .30
2 = 6.6	2 = .61
3 = 9.8	3 = .92
4 = 13.1	4 = 1.2
5 = 16.4	5 = 1.5
6 = 19.7	6 = 1.8
7 = 23.0	7 = 2.1
8 = 26.2	8 = 2.4

In This Chapter

nightlife and the arts

MOST NIGHTLIFE IN COPENHAGEN is concentrated in the area in and around Strøget, though there are student and "leftist" cafés and bars in Nørrebro and more upscale spots in Østerbro. Vesterbro, whose main drags are Vesterbrogade and Istedgade, is a budding nighttime neighborhood, with a clutch of hip bars and cafés.

The most complete English calendar of events is listed in the tourist magazine *Copenhagen This Week*, and includes musical and theatrical events as well as films and exhibitions.

NIGHTLIFE

Many restaurants, cafés, bars, and clubs stay open after midnight, a few until 5 AM. Copenhagen used to be famous for jazz, but unfortunately that has changed in recent years, with many of the best clubs closing down. However, you can find nightspots catering to almost all musical tastes, from bop to ballroom music to house, rap, and techno, in trendy clubs soundtracked by local DJs. The area around Nikolaj Kirken has the highest concentration of trendy discos and dance spots. Copenhagen's clubs can be a fickle bunch; new nighttime venues crop up regularly, often replacing last year's red-hot favorite. Call ahead or check out *Copenhagen This Week* for current listings. The stylish, biannual magazine *Copenhagen Living* (Dkr 59) includes informative listings on the latest bars, restaurants, and shops. It also features articles on Danish culture, food, and architecture and is available at stores, hotels, and the tourist office.

Bars and Lounges

The 1730s **HVIIDS VINSTUE** (Kongens Nytorv 19, tel. 33/15–10–64) attracts all kinds, young and old, singles and couples, for a glass of wine or cognac. The **LIBRARY** (Bernstorffsg. 4, tel. 33/14–15–19), in the Plaza, is an elegant spot for a quiet but pricey drink. **PEDER OXE'S** basement (Gråbrødretorv 11, tel. 33/11–11–93) is casual and young, though nearly impossible to squeeze into on weekends.

Copenhagen is peppered with hip restaurants that get even hipper in the evening, when they morph into lively nightspots. **BANG OG JENSEN** (Istedg. 130, tel. 33/25–53–18) in the spotty-but-becoming-gentrified Vesterbro neighborhood, is a regular café during the day. From 9 PM until 2 AM, however, it turns into a cocktail bar jamming with loud music and a disco ambience. **DELICATESSEN** (Vesterbrog. 120, tel. 33/22–16–33) serves international cuisine by day, but after 11 PM Thursday through Saturday, it's time for cocktails and dancing to DJ-spun house, hip-hop, and rock. At **ETC.** (Hovedvagtsg. 8, tel. 33/33–99–97), near Kongens Nytorv, Copenhagen's jet-setters sip cocktails in a pseudo-Moroccan environment, lounging on low couches and flirting around the tile bar. People start trickling in at 10 PM Friday and Saturday, and by 1 AM, it's going full swing, usually to salsa and African-inspired music. On spirited nights, revelers take to dancing between the tables. Nearby, **KONRAD** (Pilestr. 12–14, tel. 33/93–29–29) attracts a chic crowd that gathers 'round the see-and-be-seen classy bar. **CAFÉ KETCHUP** (Pilestr. 19, tel. 33/32–30–30), just off the Strøget, draws an informal—though not unsavvy—crowd that gabs and grooves to the sounds of funk, house, hip-hop, and African music. It gets cooking after 11 PM on the weekends, once cocktails start replacing coffee. Believe it or not, there are other beers in Copenhagen besides the omnipresent Carlsberg and Tuborg, and there's no better place to enjoy them than at **CHARLIE'S BAR** (Pilestr. 33, tel. 33/32–22–89), which calls itself "proudly independent, independently proud" because it doesn't serve the two biggies. Instead, you can choose from more than 46 draft and bottled beers, including a handful of Danish microbreweries and Hoegaarden beer from Belgium. This dark bar with low ceilings, owned by a transplanted Scotsman, is refreshingly unpretentious, with a laid-back crowd of regulars, from locals to expats.

The **D'ANGLETERRE HOTEL** (Kongens Nytorv 34, tel. 33/12–00–95) is home to a tiny dark-wood-and-brass bar that's just the place to soak up the posh hotel's ambience without forking over the kroner to stay here. You're in good company: the walls are lined with pics of all the famous folks who've passed through, from Eisenhower to Springsteen to a spate of aging Hollywood stars. The plus is the D'Angleterre's location right on Kongens Nytorv, which means that after a drink or two you're within close walking distance to a slew of other nighttime spots, including Victor and Konrad. For many Copenhagen old-timers, there's only one watering hole in town for a real beer, and that's the bar known only by its street number, **"90"** ("halvfems" in Danish; Gammel Kongevej 90, no phone), where it can take up to 15 minutes for the bartender to pull your draft beer. This small, atmospheric bar with dark orange walls and heavy wooden tables is the second home to a cast of crusty Copenhagen characters and outspoken barflies. At lunch, do as the locals do and buy smørrebrød from around the corner, and then bring it into the bar where you can settle in at one of the tables and enjoy your meal with one of the famous drafts. (There's a Dkr 5 charge just to sit at the table.)

Cafés

Café life appeared in Copenhagen in the '70s and quickly became a compulsory part of its urban existence. The cheapest sit-down eateries in town, where a cappuccino and sandwich often cost less than Dkr 60, cafés are lively and relaxed at night, the crowd usually interesting. About a 10-minute walk from the Østerport train station, **AMOKKO KAFFEHUS** (Dag Hammarsjolds Allé 38-40, tel. 35/25–35–36) is a coffee-lover's dream. Specialty java is served alongside inventive sandwiches and salads. **BJØRG'S** (Vester Voldg. 19, tel. 33/14–53–20) has a zinc bar, red seating, and lots of large windows. Guests slouch over huge burgers, club sandwiches, and excellent coffees. Pint-size **CCOPPA** (Pilestr. 27, tel. 33/13–00–19) may be dwarfed by the other (bigger) restaurants and stores on Pilestræde, but that's part of its charm. Consisting of little more than a counter and a handful of cube-shape tables and chairs, this snug yet stylish café—with large windows overlooking Pilestræde—serves a mean cappuccino and savory sandwiches (turkey with spicy mango chutney, or crab salad with asparagus) on wheat baguettes. **CAFÉ DAN TURRELL** (Store Regneg. 3, tel. 33/14–10–47), an old café, has of late become terribly chic, partly due its good food and candlelight. At the fashionable **EUROPA** (Amagertorv 1, tel. 33/14–28–89), people-watching and coffee naturally go together. **KRASNAPOLSKY** (Vesterg. 10, tel. 33/32–88–00) packs a young, hip, and painfully well-dressed audience at night, a more mixed group for its quiet afternoons.

Once run-down and neglected, the up-and-coming Istedgade strip is beginning to sprout cheery cafés and eateries. **MAMA LUSTRA** (Istedg. 96–98, tel. 33/25–26–11) looks like it could be a corner of your grandma's attic, with mismatched chairs, old wooden tables, and brass candle holders. Sink into a stuffed chair and sip a coffee or glass of Spanish wine while gazing out over busy Istedgade. The place also serves a simple but tasty brunch with cured ham, Italian sausages, and scrambled eggs, and an assortment of sandwiches including the vegetarian favorite—sun-dried tomatoes, pesto, and arugula. On Sunday, it hosts story-telling and spoken-word sessions. The juncture of Købmagergade and Strøget marks the Art Nouveau–style **CAFÉ NORDEN** (Østerg. 61, tel. 33/11–77–91), where substantial portions make up for minimal table space. On Nørrebro's main square, Skt. Hans Torv, the all-in-one rock club–restaurant–café **RUST** (Guldbergsg. 8, tel. 35/24–52–00) is packed all the time. Hearty, fresh dishes are served inside, and there's grill food served outside on the terrace. Come evening, **SEBASTOPOL** (Skt. Hans Torv 2, tel. 35/36–30–02) is packed with gussied-up locals. Sample the ample weekend brunch. **CAFÉ SOMMERSKO** (Kronprinsensg. 6, tel. 33/14–81–89) is the granddaddy of all the other similar places in town, with a surprisingly varied menu (try the delicious french fries with pesto or the wok specialties) and an eclectic crowd. **VICTOR** (Ny Østerg. 8, tel. 33/13–36–13) is all brass and dark wood, lovely for a light lunch.

Casino

The **CASINO COPENHAGEN** (Amager Boulevarden 70, tel. 33/11–51–15), at the SAS Scandinavia Hotel, has American and French roulette, blackjack, baccarat, and slot machines. Admission is Dkr 80 (you must be 18 years old and show a photo ID), and a dress code (jackets required; no sportswear or jeans) is enforced. The casino is open 2 PM to 4 AM.

Discos and Dancing

Most discos open at 11 PM, charging covers of about Dkr 40 as well as selling drinks at steep prices. The lively **CLUB ABSALON** (Frederiksbergg. 38, tel. 33/16–16–98), popular with nearly everyone, has live music on the ground floor and a disco above. **NASA**'s (Boltens Gård, tel. 33/93–74–15) exclusive "members only" policy has earned it legendary status among Copenhagen's nightclubs. The picky doorman decides whether or not to let you in based on his opinion of your looks, clothes, and attitude. Luckily, rumor has it that Nasa is relaxing its door policy. Once inside, you get to hobnob in a cool, white interior with the city's chic and moneyed set, local celebs (Crown Prince Frederik occasionally drops by), and usually a couple of actors and musicians who are passing through Copenhagen. Underneath

Nasa are two other clubs, Fever and Slide, with a more casual vibe and much more lax doormen. At the fashionable **PARK CAFÉ** (Østerbrog. 79, tel. 35/26–63–42), there's an old-world café with live music downstairs, a disco upstairs, and a movie theater next door. At the **RØDE PIMPERNEL** (Kattesundet 4, tel. 33/12–20–32), an adult audience gathers for dancing to live orchestras, trios, and old-time music. The very popular English-style **ROSIE MCGEES** (Vesterbrog. 2A, tel. 33/32–19–23) pub serves American and Mexican eats and encourages dancing. **SABOR LATINO** (Løngestræde 39, tel. 33/11–97–66) is the United Nations of discos, with an international crowd dancing to salsa and other Latin rhythms. The smooth **STEREO BAR** (Linnésg. 16A, tel. 33/13–61–13) has lava lamps and '70s furnishings; plays house, soul, and funk music; and draws an eclectic crowd, from design students to writers, providing your best chance for an interesting conversation in Copenhagen's club scene. **SUBSONIC** (Skinderg. 45, tel. 33/13–26–25) pulsates to '80s dance tunes and features a roomy dance floor and a reconstructed airport lounge–like area, outfitted with real airplane seats. Among the most enduring clubs is **WOODSTOCK** (Vesterg. 12, tel. 33/11–20–71), where a mixed audience grooves to music from the '50s to the '80s.

Gay Bars and Establishments

Given Denmark's long-time liberal attitudes toward homosexuality, it's not surprising that Copenhagen has a thriving and varied gay night scene. In August, Copenhagen celebrates "Mermaid Pride," its boisterous annual gay-pride parade.

The **AMIGO BAR** (Schønbergsg. 4, tel. 33/21–49–15) is popular with men of all ages. For a show-tune showdown, head for the piano bar at **CAFÉ INTIME** (Allég. 25, no phone) in Frederiksberg, where you can sip cocktails to Miss Monica's spirited renditions of standards. It's easy to meet mostly men at **CAN CAN** (Mikkel Bryggesg. 11, tel. 33/11–50–10), a small place with a friendly bartender.

The small **CENTRAL HJØRNET** (Kattesundet 18, tel. 33/11–85–49) has been around for about 70 years. The dark, casual **COSY BAR** (Studiestr. 24, tel. 33/12–74–27) is the place to go in the wee hours (it usually stays open until 8 AM). The latest addition to the gay café scene is **HEAVEN CAFÉ** (Kompagnistr. 18, tel. 33/15–19–00), which serves light meals to a casual crowd of locals and foreigners. **MASKEN** (Studiestr. 33, tel. 33/91–09–37) is a relaxed bar welcoming both men and women. The men-only **MEN'S BAR** (Teglgaardstr. 3, tel. 33/12–73–03) is dark and casual, with a leather-and-rubber dress code. Men and women pack into **PAN CLUB** (Knabrostr. 3, off Strøget, tel. 33/11–37–84), which has three floors of coffee and cocktail bars; the disco is open Wednesday through Saturday night (Dkr 40 cover). **SEBASTIAN BAR CAFÉ** (Hyskenstr. 10, tel. 33/32–22–79) is a relaxed spot for a drink or coffee. It's among the best cafés in town, with art exhibits upstairs and a bulletin board downstairs.

HOTEL WINDSOR (Frederiksborgg. 30, tel. 33/11–08–30, fax 33/11–63–87) is a gay-friendly hotel that doubles as a great diner for breakfast.

For more information, call or visit the **LANDSFORENINGEN FOR BØSSER OG LESBISKE** (Gay and Lesbian Association; Teglgaardstr. 13, Boks 1023, 1007 KBH K, tel. 33/13–19–48, www.lbl.dk/english/index.html), which has a library and more than 45 years of experience. Check out the free paper *Panbladet* for listings of nightlife events and clubs.

Jazz Clubs

Hard times have thinned Copenhagen's once-thriving jazz scene. Most of the clubs still open headline local talents, but European and international artists also perform, especially in July, when the Copenhagen Jazz Festival spills over into the clubs. Many jazz clubs host Sunday afternoon sessions that draw spirited crowds of Danes. The upscale **COPENHAGEN JAZZ HOUSE** (Niels Hemmingsensg. 10, tel. 33/15–26–00) attracts

European and some international names to its chic, modern, barlike interior. The popular Sunday afternoon jazz sessions at **DROP INN** (Kompagnistr. 34, tel. 33/11–24–04) draw a capacity crowd. This bar was designed with the audience in mind. The stage faces an informal semicircle of chairs and booths so there isn't a bad seat in the house. The eclectic decor includes wrought-iron, wreath-shape candelabras, iron statues of winged bacchanalian figures, and an M. C. Escher–style ceiling fresco. **JAZZHUSET** (Rådhusstr. 13, tel. 33/15–63–53), with exposed concrete walls decorated with local art, showcases traditional New Orleans–style jazz acts on Friday and Saturday. (It's closed on Sunday.) During the day, it functions as a café, in whose sun-lit back room you can enjoy coffee, beer, and light sandwiches. An adjoining theater features everything from Shakespeare to experimental plays. **LA FONTAINE** (Kompagnistr. 11, tel. 33/11–60–98) is Copenhagen's quintessential jazz dive, with sagging curtains, impenetrable smoke, and hep cats.

Rock Clubs

Copenhagen has a good selection of rock clubs, most of which cost less than Dkr 50. Almost all are filled with young, fashionable crowds. Clubs tend to open and go out of business with some frequency, but you can get free entertainment newspapers and flyers advertising gigs at almost any café.

BASE CAMP (Halvtolv 12, tel. 70/23–23–18) is a cavernous restaurant located in a former military hangar; after dinner, it mutates into a nightclub with live music. For good old-fashioned rock and roll, head to **LADES KÆLDER** (Kattesundet 6, tel. 33/14–00–67), a local hangout just off Strøget. The **PUMPEHUSET** (Studiestr. 52, tel. 33/93–19–60) is the place for soul and rock. **VEGA** (Engavevej 40, tel. 33/25–70–11) plays live techno, house, and rock and is a classic hangout.

THE ARTS

The most complete English calendar of events is listed in the tourist magazine *Copenhagen This Week*, and includes musical and theatrical events as well as films and exhibitions. Copenhagen's main theater and concert season runs from September through May, and tickets can be obtained either directly from theaters and concert halls or from ticket agencies. **BILLETNET** (tel. 70/15–65–65), a box-office service available at all post offices, has tickets for most major events. The main phone line is often busy; for information go in person to any post office. There's one on Købmagergade, just off Strøget. Same-day purchases at the box office at **TIVOLI** (Vesterbrog. 3, tel. 33/15–10–12) are half price if you pick them up after noon; the half-price tickets are for shows all over town, but the ticket center also has full-price tickets for the park's own performances.

Film

Films open in Copenhagen a few months to a year after their U.S. premieres. The Danes are avid viewers, willing to pay Dkr 70 per ticket, wait in lines for premieres, and read subtitles. Call the theater for reservations, and pick up tickets (which include a seat number) an hour before the movie. Most theaters have a café. Among the city's alternative venues for second-run films is **VESTER VOV VOV** (Absalonsg. 5, tel. 33/24–42–00) in Vesterbro. The **GRAND** (Mikkel Bryggersg. 8, tel. 33/15–16–11) shows new foreign and art films, and is next door to its sister café.

Opera, Ballet, and Theater

Tickets at the **KONGELIGE TEATER** (Danish Royal Theater; Tordenskjoldsg. 3, tel. 33/14–10–02) are reasonably priced at Dkr 70–Dkr 400 but, especially for prime seats, can be hard to get; the season runs October to May. It is home to the Royal Danish Ballet, one of the premier companies in the world. Not as famous, but also accomplished, are the Royal Danish Opera and

Not a Night Owl?

You can learn a lot about a place if you take its pulse after dark. So even if you're the original early-to-bed type, there's every reason to vary your routine when you're away from home.

EXPERIENCE THE FAMILIAR IN A NEW PLACE Whether your thing is going to the movies or going to concerts, it's always different away from home. In clubs, new faces and new sounds add up to a different scene. Or you may catch movies you'd never see at home.

TRY SOMETHING NEW Do something you've never done before. It's another way to dip into the local scene. A simple suggestion: Go out later than usual—go dancing late and finish up with breakfast at dawn.

DO SOMETHING OFFBEAT Look into lectures and readings as well as author appearances in book stores. You may even meet your favorite novelist.

EXPLORE A DAYTIME NEIGHBORHOOD AT NIGHT Take a nighttime walk through an explorable area you've already seen by day. You'll get a whole different view of it.

ASK AROUND If you strike up a conversation with like-minded people during the course of your day, ask them about their favorite spots. Your hotel concierge is another resource.

DON'T WING IT As soon as you've nailed down your travel dates, look into local publications or surf the Net to see what's on the calendar while you're in town. Look for hot regional acts, dance and theater, big-name performing artists, expositions, and sporting events. Then call or click to order tickets.

CHECK OUT THE NEIGHBORHOOD Whenever you don't know the neighborhood you'll be visiting, review safety issues with people in your hotel. What's the transportation situation? Can you walk there, or do you need a cab? Is there anything else you need to know?

CASH OR CREDIT? Know before you go. It's always fun to be surprised—but not when you can't cover your check.

the Royal Danish Orchestra, the latter of which performs in all productions. Plays are exclusively in Danish. For information and reservations, call the theater. Beginning at the end of July, you can order tickets for the next season by writing to the theater (Danish Royal Theater, Attn. Ticket Office, Box 2185, DK–1017 KBH). For English-language theater, especially comedy, call the professional **LONDON TOAST THEATRE** (tel. 33/22–86–86).

where to stay

COPENHAGEN IS WELL SERVED BY A WIDE RANGE OF HOTELS, overall among Europe's most expensive. The hotels around the somewhat run-down red-light district of Istedgade—which looks more dangerous than it is—are the least expensive. Copenhagen is a compact, eminently walkable city, and most of the hotels are in or near the city center, usually within walking distance of most of the major sights and thoroughfares. In summer, reservations are recommended, but should you arrive without one, try the hotel booking desk in the tourist office. It can give you a same-day, last-minute price (if available) starting at about Dkr 400 for a single hotel room. Of course, the price depends entirely on what is available. This service also finds rooms in private homes, with rates starting at about Dkr 300 for a single. It charges a fee of Dkr 50 for the service. Young travelers looking for a room or travel services should head for the student and youth budget travel agency, **HUSET/USE IT** (Rådhusstr. 13, tel. 33/73–06–20).

Breakfast is sometimes included in the room rate. Rooms have bath or shower at the following hotels unless otherwise noted. Note that in Copenhagen, as in the rest of Denmark, half (to three-fourths) of the rooms usually have showers only (while the rest have showers and bathtubs) so make sure to state your preference when booking.

CATEGORY	COST*
$$$$	over Dkr 1,700
$$$	Dkr 1,200–Dkr 1,700
$$	Dkr 700–Dkr 1,200
$	under Dkr 700

*Prices are for two people in a standard double room, including service charge and tax.

RÅDHUS PLADSEN, CHRISTIANSBORG SLOT, AND STRØGET

$$$$ RADISSON SAS SCANDINAVIA. Near the airport, this is one of northern Europe's largest hotels, and Copenhagen's token skyscraper. An immense lobby, with cool, recessed lighting and streamlined furniture, gives access to the city's first (and only) casino. Guest rooms are large and somewhat institutional but offer every modern convenience, making this a good choice if you prefer familiar comforts over character. The hotel's Top of the Town restaurant and wine bar overlook Copenhagen's copper towers and skyline. *Amager Boulevarden 70, DK–2300 KBH S, tel. 33/96–50–00, fax 33/96–55–00, www.radissonsas.com. 542 rooms, 52 suites. 4 restaurants, bar, room service, indoor pool, health club, casino, concierge, meeting room, free parking. AE, DC, MC, V.*

$$$ KONG FREDERIK. North of Rådhus Pladsen and a two-minute walk from Strøget, this intimate hotel has the same British style as its sister hotel, the D'Angleterre. The rooms are elegant, in English Colonial–style, with Asian vases, mauve carpets, and blue bedspreads. Ask for a top room for tower views. The plush restaurant Salon Frederiks serves a hearty morning buffet (not included in rates) and also lunch and dinner. *Vester Voldg. 25, DK-1552 KBH K, tel. 33/12–59–02, fax 33/93–59–01, www.remmen.dk. 110 rooms, 13 suites. Restaurant, bar, room service, meeting room, parking (fee). AE, DC, MC, V.*

$$ ASCOT. This charming downtown hotel's two outstanding features are a wrought-iron staircase and an excellent breakfast buffet. The lobby is classic, with marble and columns, but the guest rooms and apartments are comfy, with modern furniture and bright colors; some have kitchenettes. If you're going to be staying a weekend, be aware that the nearby club, Pumpehuset, blasts music until the wee hours; at least make sure your room doesn't face it. *Studiestr. 61, DK-1554 KBH K, tel. 33/12–60–00, fax 33/14–60–40, www.ascothotel.dk. 117 rooms, 45 apartments. Restaurant, bar, gym, meeting room, free parking. AE, DC, MC, V.*

$ COPENHAGEN AMAGER DANHOSTEL. This simple lodging is 4½ km (3 mi) outside town, close to the airport. The hostel is spread over nine interconnecting buildings, all laid out on one floor. International Youth Hostel members—including student backpackers as well as families—use the communal kitchen, or buy breakfast and dinner from the restaurant. The hostel is also wheelchair-accessible. Before 5 PM on weekdays, take Bus 46 from the main station directly to the hostel. After 5, from Rådhus Pladsen or the main station, take Bus 250 to Sundbyvesterplads, and change to Bus 100. Ask the driver to signal your stop. *Vejlands Allé 200, DK-2300 KBH S, tel. 32/52–29–08, fax 32/52–27–08, www.danhostel.dk/amager. 64 rooms with 2 beds, 80 family rooms with 5 beds, 4 large communal bathrooms. Restaurant. MC, V.*

AROUND AMALIENBORG AND NORTH

$$$$ D'ANGLETERRE. The grande dame of Copenhagen welcomes
★ royalty, politicians, and rock stars—from Margaret Thatcher to Madonna—in palatial surroundings: an imposing New Georgian facade leads into an English-style sitting room. Standard guest rooms are furnished in pastels, with overstuffed chairs and modern and antique furniture. The spit-and-polish staff accommodates every wish. The elegant Wiinblad restaurant serves excellent French–Danish dishes. *Kongens Nytorv 34, DK-1051 KBH K, tel. 33/12–00–95, fax 33/12–11–18, www.remmen.dk. 130 rooms, 28 suites. 2 restaurants, bar, room service, indoor pool, concierge, meeting room, parking (fee). AE, DC, MC, V.*

copenhagen lodging

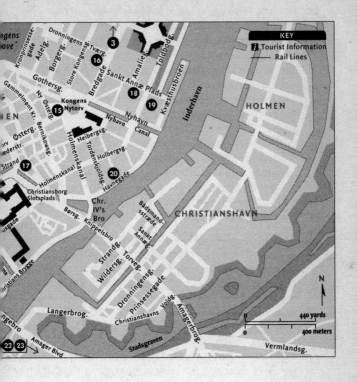

$$$ NEPTUN. This elegant, central hotel was bought years ago with the intention of making it the bohemian gathering place of Copenhagen, but these days it is more practical than artsy and welcomes business guests, tourists, and even large tour groups. The lobby and lounge are light, with classical furnishings and pale tones, and guest rooms have tasteful modern decor. Many rooms face an interior covered courtyard. Next door is the restaurant Gendarmen, run by a group of young restaurateurs who have created a dinner menu on the concept of old-meets-new, marrying traditional Danish dishes (roast pork or cod) with nouveau touches, such as a light truffle or blueberry sauce. The traditional lunch menu consists of good old Danish fare, smørrebrød and the like. Skt. Annæ Pl. 14–20, DK–1250 KBH K, tel. 33/13–89–00, fax 33/14–12–50. 133 rooms, 13 suites. Restaurant, room service, meeting room, free parking. AE, DC, MC, V.

$$$ NYHAVN 71. In a 200-year-old warehouse, this quiet, soothing hotel is a good choice for privacy-seekers. It overlooks the old ships of Nyhavn, and its nautical interiors have been preserved with their original thick plaster walls and exposed brick. The rooms are tiny but cozy, with warm woolen spreads, dark woods, soft leather furniture, and crisscrossing timbers. Avoid the wing built in 2001, since it still has some kinks that need working out. Nyhavn 71, DK–1051 KBH K, tel. 33/11–85–85, fax 33/93–15–85, www.71nyhavnhotelcopenhagen.dk. 150 rooms, 8 suites. Restaurant, bar, room service, concierge, meeting room, free parking. AE, DC, MC, V.

$$$ PHOENIX. This luxury hotel has automatic glass doors, crystal chandeliers, and gilt touches everywhere. Originally built in the 1680s, the hotel was then torn down and rebuilt into a plush, Victorian-style hotel in 1847, rising from its rubble just like the mythical Phoenix rose from its ashes, and thus its name. The suites and business-class rooms are adorned with faux antiques and 18-carat gold-plate bathroom fixtures; the standard rooms are very small, measuring barely 9 ft by 15 ft. It's so convenient to city-center attractions that the hotel gets a certain amount of street noise; light sleepers should ask for rooms above the second

When you pack your MCI Calling Card, it's like packing your loved ones along too.

Your MCI Calling Card is the easy way to stay in touch when you travel. Use it to call to and from over 125 countries. Plus, every time you call, you can earn frequent flier miles. So wherever your travels take you, call home with your MCI Calling Card. It's even easy to get one. Just visit **www.mci.com/worldphone**.

EASY TO CALL WORLDWIDE

1. **Just enter the WorldPhone® access number of the country you're calling from.**
2. **Enter or give the operator your MCI Calling Card number.**
3. **Enter or give the number you're calling.**

Australia ◆	1-800-881-100
China	108-12
France ◆	0-800-99-0019
Germany	0800-888-8000
Hong Kong	800-96-1121

Ireland	1-800-55-1001
Italy ◆	172-1022
Japan ◆	00539-121▶
South Africa	0800-99-0011
Spain	900-99-0014
United Kingdom	0800-89-0222

◆ Public phones may require deposit of coin or phone card for dial tone. ▶ Regulation does not permit intra-Japan calls.

MCI

Find America
WITH A COMPASS

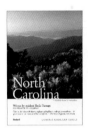
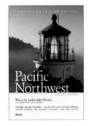

Written by local authors and illustrated throughout with
spectacular color images from regional photographers,
these companion guides reveal the character and culture
of more than 35 of America's most spectacular destinations. Perfect for residents who want to explore their own
backyards, and visitors who want an insider's perspective
on the history, heritage, and all there is to see and do.

Fodor's COMPASS AMERICAN GUIDES

At bookstores everywhere.

floor. Downstairs is Murdoch's Books & Ale, a snug pub done up in mahogany and brass, with antique Danish tomes lining its bookshelves. The pub serves smørrebrød and light meals, including a green salad topped with chicken marinated in balsamic vinegar and a ham-and-onion quiche. It's closed on Sunday. *Bredg. 37, DK–1260 KBH K, tel. 33/95–95–00, fax 33/33–98–33, www.phoenixcopenhagen.dk. 212 rooms, 7 suites. Restaurant. AE, DC, MC, V. Pub closed Sun.*

$$$ SKOVSHOVED. The delightful, art-filled inn is 8 km (5 mi) north of town, near a few old fishing cottages beside the yacht harbor. Licensed since 1660, it has retained its provincial charm. Larger rooms overlook the sea, smaller ones rim the courtyard; all have both modern and antique furnishings. *Strandvejen 267, DK–2920 Charlottenlund, tel. 39/64–00–28, fax 39/64–06–72, www.skovshoved-hotel.dk. 20 rooms, 3 suites. Restaurant, bar, meeting room. AE, DC, MC, V.*

$$ COPENHAGEN ADMIRAL. A five-minute stroll from Nyhavn, overlooking old Copenhagen and Amalienborg, the monolithic Admiral was once a grain warehouse but now affords travelers no-nonsense accommodations. With massive stone walls—broken by rows of tiny windows—it's one of the less expensive top hotels, cutting frills and prices. Its guest rooms are spare, with jutting beams and modern prints. *Toldbodg. 24–28, DK-1253 KBH K, tel. 33/74–14–14, fax 33/74–14–16, www.admiral-hotel.dk. 366 rooms, 52 suites. Restaurant, bar, sauna, nightclub, meeting room, free parking. AE, DC, MC, V.*

$$ COPENHAGEN STRAND. You can't stay closer to the harbor than here: just a five-minute walk from Nyhavn, this pleasant hotel is housed in a waterfront warehouse dating from 1869. The cozy lobby has brown leather couches and old maritime pictures on the walls. The rooms are small but comfortable, with blue and yellow bedspreads and sparkling bathrooms. *Havneg. 37, DK-1058 KBH K, tel. 33/48–99–00, fax 33/48–99–01, www.copenhagenstrand.dk. 174 rooms, 2 suites. Restaurant, bar, meeting room. AE, DC, MC, V.*

DOWN VESTERBROGADE AND NØRREBRO

$$$$ FIRST HOTEL VESTERBRO. Looming over Vesterbrogade—and just a five-minute walk from Tivoli—this four-star deluxe hotel is Denmark's third largest. The sun-drenched lobby, with floor-to-ceiling windows, has white pillars, blond-wood tables, and gray Dansk design armchairs. The rooms are equipped with all the latest gizmos, including Web TV. The rooms have pale yellow walls, cherry-wood furnishings, and contemporary lithographs. Female travelers may want try out the "First Lady" rooms, which include adjustable mirrors and makeup remover in the bathrooms, fluffy bathrobes, an electric kettle, and women's magazines. The hotel's highlight is its magnificent brick-wall atrium awash in sunlight and hanging plants, and outfitted with marble tables and rounded wicker chairs. You can also enjoy the ample complimentary breakfast buffet in the atrium. The handsome Alex Vinbar & Kokken restaurant, presided over by an up-and-coming Swedish chef, serves contemporary Scandinavian cuisine and offers more than 250 wines, any of which can be ordered by the glass. *Vesterbrog. 23–29, DK–1620 KBH V, tel. 33/78–80–00, fax 33/78–80–80, www.firsthotels.com. 403 rooms, 1 suite. Restaurant, bar, room service, concierge, meeting room, parking (fee). AE, DC, MC, V. BP.*

$$$$ PLAZA. With its convenient location and plush homey atmosphere, this hotel attracts the likes of Tina Turner and Keith Richards. Close to Tivoli and the main station, the building opens with a stately lobby and the adjacent Plaza Restaurant, with haute French–Italian cuisine. The older rooms are scattered with antiques; newer ones are furnished in a more modern style. The Library Bar is an elegantly cozy and atmospheric place for a drink, but the prices can be staggeringly high. *Bernstorffsg. 4, DK–1577 KBH V, tel. 33/14–92–62, fax 33/93–93–62, www.accorhotel.com. 93 rooms, 6 suites. Restaurant, bar, room service, concierge, meeting room, parking (fee). AE, DC, MC, V.*

$$$$ RADISSON SAS ROYAL. Towering over the heart of town, this high-rise hotel was originally designed by Arne Jacobsen in 1960.

Recently the owners spent several years—and plenty of kroner—in reembracing its Jacobsen look, and the result is a veritable paean to the legendary designer. The graceful lobby has blue and white Jacobsen swan and egg chairs that are arranged in circles and illuminated by the ceiling's recessed lights. The soothing hotel rooms are paneled in light maple and outfitted with Jacobsen chairs and lamps. Even the heavy door handles, functionally designed to fill the palm, were created by Jacobsen. The headboards are inlaid with pale green and lavender kidney shapes. The most famous room is 606, which looks just like it did in 1960, with all the original furnishings, including a nifty desktop that opens to reveal a lighted makeup mirror. Many of the rooms boast views over the city center's copper-top buildings and of Tivoli. The hotel offers an Internet center. The top-floor restaurant, Alberto K, serves top-notch Scandinavian–Italian cuisine. You don't have to be a hotel guest to bask in Jacobsen's aura. For the price of a cocktail, you can hang out in the elegant hotel bar, sitting on—and amid—Jacobsen designs. *Hammerichsg. 1, DK–1611 KBH V, tel. 33/42–60–00, fax 33/42–61–00, www.radissonsas.com. 260 rooms, 2 suites. Restaurant, bar, room service, sauna, concierge, meeting room, parking (fee). AE, DC, MC, V.*

$$$ DGI BYEN. "An unusual meeting place" is how the DGI Byen presents itself, and it's a thoroughly apt description. This state-of-the-art recreation and sports center, just behind the Central train station, boasts a bowling alley, climbing wall, shooting range, swimming pool, spa, and 104-room hotel. The hotel rooms are an exquisite blend of Danish design. Dark blue furnishings and blond-wood floors are softly illuminated by cylindrical lamps. Short poems by the much-loved Danish philosopher Piet Hein grace the cool gray walls. Though most rooms have doubly insulated windows, you can sometimes hear the distant rumble of trains entering the station. The last train passes by at around 12:30 AM, but ask for a quiet room if you're a light sleeper. The pool is free to hotel guests; nonguests pay Dkr 46. Use of the full-service spa costs extra, but here you can pamper yourself with a range of soothing treatments. Ask about the substantially lower weekend rates. *Tietgensg. 65, DK–1704 KBH V, tel. 33/29–80–00, fax 33/29–80–80, www.dgi-byen.dk. 104 rooms. Restaurant, café, pool, sauna, spa, bowling, meeting room, parking (fee). AE, DC, MC, V.*

$$$ GRAND HOTEL. In operation since the turn of the 20th century, the Grand Hotel has a faded elegance that can be comforting. From its old-style lobby, presided over by a crystal chandelier, to its narrow stairs and uneven hallways, this hotel stands as the proud antithesis to all that's sleek and shiny. The rooms are a blend of old and new, with blue-and-gold curtains, traditional cherry-wood furnishings, and all the modern conveniences, such as satellite TVs and minibars. The drawback is that some of the rooms have tiny bathrooms, so inquire about this when booking. *Vesterbrog. 9, DK–1620 KBH V, tel. 33/27–69–00, fax 33/27–69–01, www.grandhotelcopenhagen.dk. 161 rooms, 3 suites. Restaurant, bar, room service, concierge, meeting room, parking (fee). AE, DC, MC, V.*

$$$ SCANDIC COPENHAGEN. Rising over Copenhagen's lakes, alongside the cylindrical Tycho Brahe Planetarium, is this modern high-rise hotel. The comfortable rooms, done up in cool tones and blond-wood furnishings, have splendid views. One side of the hotel overlooks the peaceful lakes, and the other side the bustling heart of Copenhagen, including Tivoli. The higher up you go, the better the view, so inquire about a room on the 17th floor, which is the highest floor that still has standard doubles; it's suites-only on the 18th floor. *Vester Søg. 6, DK–1601 KBH V, tel. 33/14–35–35, fax 33/31–12–23, www.scandic-hotels.com. 472 rooms, 6 suites. Restaurant, bar, room service, sauna, gym, concierge, meeting room, parking (fee). AE, DC, MC, V.*

$$ COPENHAGEN CROWN. Tucked into a small brick courtyard just off busy Vesterbrogade, this simple hotel has small but comfortable rooms with pale yellow walls and light green curtains. Some rooms overlook Vesterbrogade and the rest face the interior courtyard. The rooftop breakfast room floods with sunlight during the summer and offers pleasant bird's-eye views of the Vesterbro neighborhood. *Vesterbrog. 41, DK–1620 KBH V, tel. 33/21–21–66, fax 33/21–00–66, www.phg.dk. 80 rooms. Meeting rooms, parking (fee). AE, DC, MC, V.*

$$ IBSENS HOTEL. This winsome, family-owned hotel near the Nørreport station has cozy, immaculate rooms and a lovely courtyard. The friendly staff is particularly attentive and will go out of its way to help. This attention to detail is evident in the hotel's decor, as well. Each floor has its own theme. The Scandinavian floor showcases cool and modern local designs while the Bohemian floor is filled with antique furnishings. The breakfast room is a lovely place to start your morning. *Vendersg. 23, DK–1363 KBH K, tel. 33/13–19–13, fax 33/12–19–16, www.ibsenshotel.dk. 105 rooms, 5 suites. Bar, parking (fee). AE, DC, MC, V.*

$$ TRITON. Despite seedy surroundings, this streamlined hotel attracts a cosmopolitan clientele thanks to a central location in Vesterbro. The large rooms, in blond wood and warm tones, all include modern bathroom fixtures. The buffet breakfast is exceptionally generous and the staff friendly. There are also family rooms with a bedroom and a dining–sitting area with a sofabed. *Helgolandsg. 7–11, DK-1653 KBH K, tel. 33/31–32–66, fax 33/31–69–70, www.accorhotel.com. 123 rooms, 6 family rooms. Bar, meeting room. AE, DC, MC, V.*

$ CAB–INN SCANDINAVIA. This bright hotel is just west of the lakes and Vesterport Station. Its impeccably maintained rooms are distinctly small, but designed with super efficiency to include ample showers, fold-away and bunk beds, and even electric water kettles. The hotel is popular with business travelers in winter and kroner-pinching backpackers and families in summer. Its sister hotel, the **Cab–Inn Copenhagen** (tel. 33/21–04–00, 33/21–74–09) is just around the corner, at Danasvej 32–34, but it's open only from April through September. *Vodroffsvej 55–57, DK-1900 Frederiksberg, tel. 35/36–11–11, fax 35/36–11–14, www.cab-inn.dk. 201 rooms. Breakfast room, snack bar, meeting room. AE, DC, MC, V.*

Hotel How-Tos

Where you stay does make a difference. Do you prefer a modern high-rise or an intimate B&B? A center-city location or the quiet suburbs? What facilities do you want? Sort through your priorities, then price it all out.

HOW TO GET A DEAL After you've chosen a likely candidate or two, phone them directly and price a room for your travel dates. Then call the hotel's toll-free number and ask the same questions. Also try consolidators and hotel-room discounters. You won't hear the same rates twice. On the spot, make a reservation as soon as you are quoted a price you want to pay.

PROMISES, PROMISES If you have special requests, make them when you reserve. Get written confirmation of any promises.

SETTLE IN Upon arriving, make sure everything works—lights and lamps, TV and radio, sink, tub, shower, and anything else that matters. Report any problems immediately. And don't wait until you need extra pillows or blankets or an ironing board to call housekeeping. Also check out the fire emergency instructions. Know where to find the fire exits, and make sure your companions do, too.

IF YOU NEED TO COMPLAIN Be polite but firm. Explain the problem to the person in charge. Suggest a course of action. If you aren't satisfied, repeat your requests to the manager. Document everything: Take pictures and keep a written record of who you've spoken with, when, and what was said. Contact your travel agent, if he made the reservations.

KNOW THE SCORE When you go out, take your hotel's business cards (one for everyone in your party). If you have extras, you can give them out to new acquaintances who want to call you.

TIP UP FRONT For special services, a tip or partial tip in advance can work wonders.

USE ALL THE HOTEL RESOURCES A concierge can make difficult things easy. But a desk clerk, bellhop, or other hotel employee who's friendly, smart, and ambitious can often steer you straight as well. A gratuity is in order if the advice is helpful.

$ MISSIONHOTELLET NEBO. Though it's between the main train station and Istedgade's seediest porn shops, this budget hotel is still prim, comfortable, and well maintained by a friendly staff. Its dormlike guest rooms, of which fewer than half have a bathroom, are furnished with industrial carpeting, polished pine furniture, and plain duvet covers. Baths, showers, and toilets are at the center of each hallway, and downstairs there's a sunny breakfast restaurant with a tiny courtyard. *Istedg. 6, DK-1650 KBH V, tel. 33/21–12–17, fax 33/23–47–74, www.nebo.dk. 96 rooms, 35 with bath. AE, DC, MC, V.*

AIRPORT

$$$$ HILTON COPENHAGEN AIRPORT. Half the rooms at this business hotel have views of the city's skyline; the other half look out onto the airport. Rooms are done in a modern Scandinavian style. *Copenhagen Airport, Ellehammersvej 20, DK-2770, tel. 32/50–15–01, fax 32/52–85–28, www.hiltonhotels.com. 382 rooms, 8 suites. 3 restaurants, bar, pool, sauna, gym, conference rooms. AE, DC, MC, V.*

In This Chapter

side trips

WITHIN EASY REACH OF COPENHAGEN, these side trips allow you to trade in the urban environment for the beauty of the Danish countryside. Visit affluent seaside towns with chic beaches; picture-perfect islands; fields dotted with half-timber cottages; country art museums; and rustic inns.

EXPERIMENTARIUM

8 km (5 mi) north of Copenhagen.

In the beachside town of Hellerup is the user-friendly **EXPERIMENTARIUM,** where more than 300 exhibitions are clustered in various Discovery Islands, each exploring a different facet of science, technology, and natural phenomena. A dozen body- and hands-on exhibits allow you to take skeleton-revealing bike rides, measure your lung capacity, stir up magnetic goop, play ball on a jet stream, and gyrate to gyroscopes. Once a bottling plant for the Tuborg Brewery, this center organizes one or two special exhibits a year; past installations have included interactive exhibits of the brain and tongue-wagging, life-size dinosaurs. Take Bus 6 or 650S from Rådhus Pladsen or the S-train to Hellerup; transfer to bus 21 or 650S. Alternatively, take the S-train to Svanemøllen station, then walk north for 10 minutes. *Tuborg Havnevej 7, tel. 39/27–33–33, www.experimentarium.dk. Dkr 85; combined admission for a child and parent, Dkr 120. Mid-Aug.–mid-June, Mon. and Wed.–Fri. 9–5, Tues. 9–9, weekends 11–5; mid-June–mid-Aug., daily 10–5.*

CHARLOTTENLUND

10 km (6 mi) north of Copenhagen (take Bus 6 from Rådhus Pladsen or S-train to Charltennlund station).

Just north of Copenhagen is the leafy, affluent coastal suburb of Charlottenlund, with a small, appealing beach that gets predictably crowded on sunny weekends. A little farther north is **CHARLOTTENLUND SLOT** (Charlottenlund Palace), a graceful mansion that has housed various Danish royals since the 17th century. Today, it houses only offices and is not open to the public. The surrounding peaceful palace gardens, however, are open to all, and Copenhageners enjoy coming up here for weekend ambles and picnics.

A favorite with families is the nearby **DANMARKS AKVARIUM** (Danmarks Aquarium), a sizeable, well-designed aquarium near the palace with all the usual aquatic suspects, from gliding sharks to brightly colored tropical fish to snapping crocodiles. *Kvalergården 1, tel. 39/62–32–83, www.danmarks-akvarium.dk. Dkr 60. Mid-Oct.–mid-Feb., weekdays 10–4, weekends 10–5; mid-Feb.–mid-Oct., daily 10–6.*

★ While in Charlottenlund, don't miss the remarkable **ORDRUPGAARD,** one of the largest museum collections of French impressionism in Europe outside of France. Most of the great 19th-century French artists are represented, including Manet, Monet, Matisse, Cezanne, Renoir, Degas, Gauguin, Alfred Sisley, Delacroix, and Pissarro. Particularly noteworthy is Delacroix's 1838 painting of George Sand. The original painting depicted George Sand listening to her lover Chopin play the piano. For unknown reasons, the painting was divided, and the half portraying Chopin now hangs in the Louvre. The Ordrupgaard also has a superb collection of Danish Golden Age painters, from Christen Købke to Vilhelm Hammershøj, who has been called "the Danish Edward Hopper" because of the deft use of light and space in his haunting, solitary paintings. Perhaps best of all is that much of the magnificent collection is displayed, refreshingly, in a non-museumlike setting. The paintings hang on the walls of what was once the home of museum founder and art collector Wilhelm Hansen. The lovely interior of this graceful manor house dating from 1918 has been left just as it was when Hansen and his wife, Henny, lived here. The white-and-gold ceiling has intricate flower moldings, and the gleaming dark-wood tables are set with Royal Copenhagen Flora Danica porcelain. Interspersed among the paintings are windows that provide glimpses of the surrounding lush, park-size grounds of beech trees, sloping lawns, a rose garden, and an orchard. Note that the museum may be closed for renovations, so call ahead. *Vilvordevej 110, tel. 39/64–11–83, www. ordrupgaard.dk. Dkr 25 (Dkr 50 for special exhibits). Tues.–Sun. 1–5.*

NEED A BREAK? Before or after your visit to the Ordrupgaard museum, wind down next door at the soothing **ORDRUPGAARD CAFÉ** (Vilvordevej 110, Chartlottenlund, 39/64–11–83), housed in the former stable of the manor house–turned–museum. Large picture windows overlook the wooded grounds, and museum posters of French and Danish artists line the café's whitewashed walls. Sink into one of the rustic cane chairs and enjoy the daily changing menu of light Danish–French dishes, such as the smoked salmon drizzled with lime sauce or a fluffy ham quiche served with fresh greens. For an afternoon snack, try a pastry along with a pot of coffee that you can refill as often as you wish. On Sunday from noon to 2, it serves a hearty brunch of eggs, bacon, smoked ham, and rye bread. The café is open Tuesday through Sunday, noon–5. Credit cards are not accepted.

DRAGØR

22 km (14 mi) east of Copenhagen (take Bus 30 or 33 from Rådhus Pladsen).

On the island of Amager, less than a half hour from Copenhagen, the quaint fishing town of Dragør (pronounced *drah*-wer) feels far away in distance and time. The town is set apart from the rest of the area around Copenhagen because it was settled by Dutch farmers in the 16th century. King Christian II ordered the community to provide fresh produce and flowers for the royal court. Today, neat rows of terra-cotta–roof houses trimmed with wandering ivy, roses, and the occasional waddling goose characterize the still meticulously maintained community. If there's one color that characterizes Dragør, it's the lovely pale yellow (called Dragør Gul, or Dragør yellow) of its houses. According to local legend, the former town hall's chimney was built with a twist so that meetings couldn't be overheard.

As you're wandering around Dragør, notice that many of the older houses have an angled mirror contraption attached to their street-level windows. This *gade spejl* (street mirror), unique to Scandinavia, was—and perhaps still is—used by the occupants of the house to "spy" on the street activity. Usually positioned at seat-level, this is where the curious (often the older ladies of town) could pull up a chair and observe all the comings and goings of the neighborhood from the warmth and privacy of their own homes. You can see these street mirrors all across Denmark's small towns and sometimes in the older neighborhoods of the bigger cities.

The **DRAGØR MUSEUM,** in one of the oldest houses in town, sits near the water on Dragør's colorful little harbor. The collection includes furniture from old skipper houses, costumes, drawings, and model ships. The museum shop has a good range of books on Dragør's history. *Havnepladsen, tel. 32/53–41–06, www. dragor-information.dk. Dkr 20. May–Sept., Tues.–Fri. 2–5, weekends noon–6.*

A ticket to the Dragør Museum also affords entrance to the **MØLSTED MUSEUM,** which displays paintings by the famous local artist Christian Mølsted, whose colorful canvases capture the maritime ambience of Dragør and its rich natural surroundings. *Dr. Dichs Pl. 4, tel. 32/53–41–06. Dkr 20. May–Aug., weekends 2–5.*

You can swing by the **AMAGER MUSEUM** in the nearby village of Store Magleby, 2 km (1 mi) west of Dragør. The museum is housed in two thatch-roof, whitewashed vintage farmhouses, which were once the home of the Dutch farmers and their families who settled here in the 16th century. The farmhouses are done up in period interiors, with original furnishings and displays of traditional Dutch costumes. Round out your visit with an outdoor stroll past grazing dairy cows and through well-tended vegetable gardens flourishing with the same vegetables that the settlers grew. *Hovedg. 4 and 12, tel. 32/53–02–50. Dkr 20. May–Sept., Tues.–Fri. noon–4; Oct.–Apr., Wed. and Sun. noon–4.*

Dining and Lodging

$$$ RESTAURANT BEGHUSET. This handsome restaurant with rustic stone floors and green-and-gold painted doors is named Beghuset (Pitch House), because this is where Dragør's fishermen used to boil the pitch that waterproofed their wooden ships. The creative Danish cuisine includes fried pigeon with mushrooms, grapes, and potatoes drizzled with a thyme and balsamic vinegar dressing. The front-room café was once an old dry-foods store, hence all the old wooden shelves and drawers behind the bar. Here you can order simple (and inexpensive) dishes such as a beef patty with onions and baked potatoes, and wash them down with a cold beer. *Strandg. 14, tel. 32/53–01–36. DC, MC, V. Closed Mon.*

$$ DRAGØR STRANDHOTEL. Dragør's harborside centerpiece is this spacious, sunny restaurant and café, its exterior awash in a cool yellow, like so many of the buildings in town. The Strandhotel started life as an inn, nearly 700 years ago, making it one of Denmark's oldest inns. Danish royalty used to stay here in the 1500s, after going swan hunting nearby, and in the 1800s, Søren Kierkegaard was a regular guest. Though it has kept the "hotel" in its name, today it is only a restaurant. Owned and run by the

Helgstrand family for the past 25 years, the Strandhotel has retained its former charms—vintage wooden cupboards and colored ceramics—with views of Dragør's small, bustling harbor. The menu is, disappointingly, tourist-driven (with items such as Mexi-burgers and Caesar salads), but the restaurant also serves Danish fare, including *frikadeller* (pork meatballs) with potato salad; fillet of sole with *remoulade* (a creamy sauce); and cod with red beets, mustard sauce, and chopped boiled egg. *Havnen, tel. 32/52–00–75. DC, MC, V. Closed Nov.–Mar.*

$$ **DRAGØR BADEHOTEL.** Built in 1907 as a seaside hotel for vacationing Copenhageners, this plain, comfortable hotel is still geared to the summer crowds, yet manages to maintain its wonderfully low prices (you'd easily pay twice the price in Copenhagen). The basic rooms have dark green carpets and simple furniture; half the rooms include little terraces that face toward the water, so make sure to ask for one when booking. The bathrooms are small and basic, with a shower only (no bathtubs). Breakfast, which is included in the price, is served on the outside terrace during the summer. *Drogdensvej 43, Dragør 2791, tel. 32/53–05–00, fax 32/53–04–99. 35 rooms. Restaurant, meeting room. AE, DC, MC, V.*

KLAMPENBORG, BAKKEN, AND DYREHAVEN

15 km (9 mi) north of Copenhagen (take Bus 6 from Rådhus Pladsen or S-train to Klampenborg station).

As you follow the coast north of Copenhagen, you'll come upon the wealthy enclave of Klampenborg, whose residents are lucky enough to have the pleasant **BELLEVUE BEACH** nearby. In summer, this luck may seem double-edged, when scores of city-weary sun-seekers pile out at the Klampenborg S-train station and head for the sand. The Danes have a perfect word for this: they call Bellevue a *fluepapir* (flypaper) beach. Still and all, Bellevue is an appealing seaside spot to soak up some rays, especially considering that it's just a 20-minute train ride from Copenhagen.

Klampenborg is no stranger to crowds. Just a few kilometers inland, within the peaceful **Dyrehaven**, is **BAKKEN**, the world's oldest amusement park—and one of Denmark's most popular attractions. If Tivoli is champagne in a fluted glass, then Bakken is a pint of beer. Bakken's crowd is working-class Danes, and lunch is hot dogs and cotton candy. Of course, Tivoli, with its trimmed hedges, dazzling firework displays, and evening concerts is still Copenhagen's reigning queen, but unpretentious Bakken makes no claims to the throne; instead, it is unabashedly about having a good time—being silly in the bumper cars, screaming at the top of your lungs on the rides, and eating food that's bad for you. There's something comfortable and nostalgic about Bakken's vaguely dilapidated state. Bakken has more than 100 rides, from quaint, rickety roller coasters (refreshingly free of that Disney gloss) to newer, faster rides to little-kid favorites such as Kaffekoppen, the Danish version of twirling teacups, where you sit in traditional Royal Copenhagen–style blue-and-white coffee cups. Bakken opens in the last weekend in March, with a festive ride by motorcyclists across Copenhagen to Bakken. It closes in late August, because this is when the Dyrehaven park animals begin to mate, and during this raging hormonal stage, the animals can be dangerous around children. *Dyrehavevej 62, inside Dyrhaven (take S-train to Klampenborg Station), tel. 39/63–35–44, www.bakken.dk. Free; rides cost Dkr 10–Dkr 25. Late Mar.–late Aug., noon–midnight.*

★ Bakken sits within the verdant, 2,500-acre **DYREHAVEN** (Deer Park), where herds of wild deer roam freely. Once the favored hunting grounds of Danish royals, today Dyrehaven has become a cherished weekend oasis for Copenhageners. Hiking and biking trails traverse the park, and lush fields beckon to nature-seekers and families with picnic hampers. The deer are everywhere; in the less-trafficked regions of the park, you may find yourself surrounded by an entire herd of deer delicately stepping through the fields. The park's centerpiece is the copper-top, 17th-century **Eremitagen,** formerly a royal hunting lodge. It is closed to the public. Today, the Royal Hunting Society gathers here for annual lunches and celebrations, most famously on the first Sunday in November, when the society hosts a popular (and televised) horseback-riding obstacle course through the park. The wet and muddy finale takes place near the Eremitagen when the riders attempt to make it across a small lake. Dyrehaven is a haven for hikers and bikers, but you can also go in for the royal treatment and enjoy it from the high seat of a horse-drawn carriage. The carriages gather at the park entrance near the Klampenborg S-train station. The cost is Dkr 40 for 15 minutes, Dkr 60 to Bakken, and Dkr 250 to the Eremitagen. *Park entrance is near Klampenborg S-train station, tel. 39/63–00–01.*

Dining

$$$$ **STRANDMØLLEKROEN.** The 200-year-old beachfront inn is filled
★ with antiques and hunting trophies. The best views are of the Øresund from the back dining room. Elegantly served seafood and steaks are the mainstays, and for a bit of everything, try the seafood platter, with lobster, crab claws, and Greenland shrimp. *Strandvejen 808, Klampenborg, tel. 39/63–01–04. AE, DC, MC, V.*

FRILANDSMUSEET

16 km (10 mi) north of Copenhagen.

North of Copenhagen is Lyngby, its main draw the **FRILANDSMUSEET,** an open-air museum. About 50 farmhouses and cottages representing various periods of Danish history have been painstakingly dismantled, moved here, reconstructed, and filled with period furniture and tools. Trees and gardens surround the museum; bring lunch and plan to spend the day. To get here, take the S-train to the Sorgenfri Station, then walk right and follow the signs. *100 Kongevejen, Lyngby, tel. 45/85–02–92, www.natmus.dk. Dkr 40; free Wed. Easter–Sept., Tues.–Sun. 10–5; Oct., Tues.–Sun. 10–4; call to confirm Oct. hrs.*

MUSEET FOR MODERNE KUNST (ARKEN)
20 km (12 mi) south of Copenhagen (take the S-train in the direction of either Hundige, Solrød Strand, or Køge to Ishøj Station, then pick up Bus 128 to the museum).

Architect Søren Robert Lund was just 25 when awarded the commission for this forward-looking museum, which he designed in metal and white concrete set against the flat coast south of Copenhagen. The museum, also known as the Arken, opened in March 1996 to great acclaim, both for its architecture and its collection. Unfortunately, for about two years following its opening, it was plagued with a string of stranger-than-fiction occurrences, including a director with an allegedly bogus resume. The situation has greatly improved and today the museum's massive sculpture room exhibits both modern Danish and international art, as well as experimental works. Dance, theater, film, and multimedia exhibits are additional attractions. *Skovvej 42 Ishøj, tel. 43/42–02–22, www.arken.dk. Dkr 50. Tues. and Thurs.–Sun. 10–5, Wed. 10–9.*

practical information

Air Travel to and from Copenhagen

BOOKING

When you book look for nonstop flights and remember that "direct" flights stop at least once. Try to avoid connecting flights, which require a change of plane. For more booking tips and to check prices and make on-line flight reservations, log on to www.fodors.com.

CARRIERS

SAS, the main carrier, makes nonstop flights to Copenhagen from Chicago, Newark, and Seattle. British Airways offers connecting flights via London from Atlanta, Baltimore, Boston, Charlotte, Chicago, Dallas, Denver, Detroit, Houston, Los Angeles, Miami, New York, Orlando, Philadelphia, Phoenix, Pittsburgh, San Diego, San Francisco, Seattle, Tampa, and Washington, D.C. Icelandair makes connecting flights via Reykjavík from Baltimore, Fort Lauderdale, New York, and Orlando. Finnair has service through Helsinki from Miami, New York, and—between May and September—San Francisco.

British Airways flies nonstop from Heathrow, Gatwick, Birmingham, and Manchester. SAS Scandinavian Airlines flies nonstop from Heathrow, Manchester, and Glasgow and also from London to Århus. Aer Lingus flies direct from Dublin. Mærsk Air flies nonstop from Gatwick to Copenhagen. Go Fly Ltd. has very cheap flights between London's Stansted airport and Copenhagen. Virgin Airlines is also inexpensive and flies between London's Gatwick and Stansted airports via Brussels to Copenhagen.

➤ **AIRLINES AND CONTACTS: Aer Lingus** (tel. 0161/832–5771 in Ireland). **Air France** (tel. 33/12–76–76 in Copenhagen). **British Airways** (tel. 80/20–80–22 in Copenhagen; tel. 0207/491–4989 in the U.K.; 800/247–9297 in the U.S.). **Delta** (tel. 800/221–1212 in the U.S.; www.delta.com). **Finnair** (tel. 800/950–5000 in the U.S.). **Go Fly Ltd.** (tel. 0845/6054–321 in the U.K.). **Icelandair** (tel. 33/12–33–88 in Copenhagen; tel. 800/223–5500 in the U.S.). **Mærsk Air** (tel. 0207/333–0066 in Copenhagen). **SAS Scandinavian Airlines** (tel. 32/32–00–00 in Copenhagen; tel. 0207/706–8832 in the U.K.; 800/221–2350 in the U.S.). **Virgin Airlines** (tel. 0207/744–00046 in the U.K.).

CHECK-IN & BOARDING

Always ask your carrier about its check-in policy. Plan to arrive at the airport about two hours before your scheduled departure time for domestic flights and 2½ to 3 hours before international flights.

Always bring a government-issued photo I.D. to the airport; even when it's not required, a passport is best.

CUTTING COSTS

The SAS Visit Scandinavia/Europe Air Pass offers up to eight flight coupons for one-way travel within and between Scandinavian cities (and participating European cities such as Frankfurt, Paris, and London). Most one-way tickets for domestic travel within each Scandinavian country cost $65; one-way fares between Scandinavian countries are usually $75, unless you are venturing into the far north, Lapland, Iceland, or Greenland (these flights range from $115 to $225). These passes can only be bought by non-Scandinavians, in conjunction with a roundtrip ticket between North America and Europe on SAS and must be used within three months of arrival. SAS also provides family fares—children between 2 and 17 and a spouse can receive 50%

off the full fare of business class tickets with the purchase of one full-fare business class ticket. Contact SAS for information.

The least expensive airfares to Scandinavia must usually be purchased in advance and are non-refundable. It's smart to **call a number of airlines,** and when you are quoted a good price, **book it on the spot**—the same fare may not be available the next day. Always **check different routings** and look into using different airports. Travel agents, especially low-fare specialists (☞ Discounts & Deals), are helpful.

Consolidators are another good source. They buy tickets for scheduled international flights at reduced rates from the airlines, then sell them at prices that beat the best fare available directly from the airlines, usually without restrictions. Sometimes you can even get your money back if you need to return the ticket. Carefully read the fine print detailing penalties for changes and cancellations, and **confirm your consolidator reservation with the airline.**

➤ **CONSOLIDATORS: Cheap Tickets** (tel. 800/377–1000). **Discount Airline Ticket Service** (tel. 800/576–1600). **Unitravel** (tel. 800/325–2222). **Up & Away Travel** (tel. 212/889–2345). **World Travel Network** (tel. 800/409–6753).

ENJOYING THE FLIGHT

For more legroom, **request an emergency-aisle seat.** Don't sit in the row in front of the emergency aisle or in front of a bulkhead, where seats may not recline. If you have dietary concerns, **ask for special meals when booking.** These can be vegetarian, low-cholesterol, or kosher, for example. On long flights, try to maintain a normal routine, to help fight jet lag. At night, get some sleep. By day, **eat light meals, drink water** (not alcohol), and **move around the cabin** to stretch your legs. For additional jet-lag tips consult *Fodor's FYI: Travel Fit & Healthy* (available at bookstores everywhere).

FLYING TIMES

From London to Copenhagen the flight takes 1 hour, 55 minutes. From New York, flights to Copenhagen take 7 hours, 40 minutes. From Chicago, they take 9 hours, 30 minutes. From Seattle and Los Angeles the flight time is about 10 hours, 55 minutes.

HOW TO COMPLAIN

If your baggage goes astray or your flight goes awry, complain right away. Most carriers require that you **file a claim immediately.**

➤ **AIRLINE COMPLAINTS: U.S. Department of Transportation Aviation Consumer Protection Division** (C-75, Room 4107, Washington, DC 20590, tel. 202/366–2220, www.dot.gov/airconsumer). **Federal Aviation Administration Consumer Hotline** (tel. 800/322–7873).

Airports & Transfers

Kastrup International Airport, the hub of Scandinavian air travel, is 10 km (6 mi) southeast of downtown Copenhagen.

➤ **AIRPORT INFORMATION: Kastrup International Airport** (tel. 45/32–31–32–31, www.cph.dk).

TRANSFERS

Although the 10-km (6-mi) drive from the airport to downtown is quick and easy, public transportation is excellent and much cheaper than other options. The airport's sleek subterranean train system takes less than 12 minutes to zip passengers into Copenhagen's main train station. Buy a ticket upstairs (Dkr 19.50); there are three trains an hour into Copenhagen, while a fourth travels further to Roskilde. Trains also travel from the airport directly to Malmö, Sweden, via the Øresund Bridge. Trains run every 20 minutes on weekdays from about 5 AM to around midnight. On Saturday, trains run from around 6 AM to midnight, and on Sunday from 6 AM to around 11 PM. The trip takes 35 minutes, and costs Dkr 60.

SAS coach buses leave the international arrivals terminal every 15 minutes, from about 5:42 AM to about 9:45 PM, cost Dkr 40, and take 25 minutes to reach Copenhagen's main train station on Vesterbrogade. Another SAS coach from Christiansborg, on Slotsholmsgade, to the airport runs every 15 minutes between 8:30 AM and noon, and every half-hour from noon to 6 PM. HT city buses depart from the international arrivals terminal every 15 minutes, from 4:30 AM (Sunday 5:30 AM) to 11:52 PM, but take a long, circuitous route. Take Bus 250S for the Rådhus Pladsen and transfer. One-way tickets cost about Dkr 20.

The 20-minute taxi ride downtown costs from Dkr 100 to Dkr 160 and up. Lines form at the international arrivals terminal. In the unlikely event there is no taxi available, there are several taxi companies you can call including Kobenhavns Taxa.

➤ **TAXIS: Kobenhavns Taxa** (tel. 35/35–35–35).

Bike Travel

Bikes are delightfully well suited to Copenhagen's flat terrain and are popular among Danes as well as visitors. Bike rental costs Dkr 35–Dkr 70 a day, with a deposit of Dkr 100–Dkr 300. You may also be lucky enough to find a free city bike chained up at bike racks in various spots throughout the city, including Nørreport and Nyhavn. Insert a Dkr 20 coin, which will be returned to you when you return the bike.

➤ **BIKE RENTALS: Københavns Cycler** (Reventlowsg. 11, tel. 33/33–86–13). **Østerport Cykler** (Oslo Plads, tel. 33/33–85–13). **Urania Cykler** (Gammel Kongevej 1, tel. 33/21–80–88).

BIKES IN FLIGHT

Most airlines accommodate bikes as luggage, provided they are dismantled and boxed. Airlines sell bike boxes, which are often free at bike shops, for about $5 (it's at least $100 for bike bags). International travelers can sometimes substitute a bike for a piece of checked luggage at no charge; otherwise, the cost is about $100. Domestic and Canadian airlines charge $25–$50.

Boat & Ferry Travel

Frequent ferries connect Copenhagen with Sweden, including several daily ships from Malmö, Limhamn, Landskrona, and Helsingborg. There is also a high-speed craft from Malmö.

Scandinavian Seaways Ferries (DFDS) sail from Harwich in the United Kingdom to Esbjerg (20 hours) on Jylland's west coast. Schedules in both summer and winter are very irregular. There are many discounts, including 20% for senior citizens and the disabled, and 50% for children between the ages of 4 and 16. For car ferry information, *see* Car Travel. The ScanRail Pass, for travel anywhere within Scandinavia (Denmark, Sweden, Norway, and Finland), and the Interail and EurailPasses are valid on some ferry crossings. Call the DSB Travel Office for information.

➤ **BOAT AND FERRY INFORMATION: DSB** (tel. 33/14–17–01 or 42/52–92–22). **Scandinavian Seaways Ferries** (DFDS; Skt. Annæ Plads 30, DK-1295 Copenhagen, tel. 33/15–63–00).

Bus Travel to and from Copenhagen

Not particularly comfortable or fast, bus travel is inexpensive. Eurolines travels from London's Victoria Station on Saturday at 2:30 PM, crossing the North Sea on the Dover-Calais ferry, and arrives in Copenhagen about 22 hours later.

CUTTING COSTS
Eurolines offers 15-, 30-, and 60-day passes for unlimited travel between Stockholm, Copenhagen, and Oslo, and over 20 destinations throughout Europe.

➤ **BUS INFORMATION: Eurolines** (52 Grosvenor Gardens, SW1, London, tel. 0207/730–8235; Copenhagen office Reventlowsg. 8, DK–1651, tel. 33/25–12–44).

Business Hours

BANKS AND OFFICES

Banks in Copenhagen are open weekdays 9:30 to 4 and Thursdays until 6. Several *bureaux de change*, including the ones at Copenhagen's central station and airport, stay open until 10 PM. Outside Copenhagen, banking hours vary.

MUSEUMS AND SIGHTS

A number of Copenhagen's museums hold confounding hours, so always call first to confirm. As a rule, however, most museums are open 10 to 3 or 11 to 4 and are closed on Monday. In winter, opening hours are shorter, and some museums close for the season. Check the local papers or ask at tourist offices for current schedules.

SHOPS

Though many Danish stores are expanding their hours, sometimes even staying open on Sunday, most shops still keep the traditional hours: weekdays 10 to 5:30, until 7 on Thursday and Friday, until 1 or 2 on Saturday—though the larger department stores stay open until 5. Everything except bakeries, kiosks, flower shops, and a handful of grocers are closed on Sunday, and most bakeries take Monday off. The first and last Saturday of the month are Long Saturdays, when even the smaller shops, especially in large cities, stay open until 4 or 5. Grocery stores stay open until 8 PM on weekdays, and kiosks until much later.

Cameras & Photography

The *Kodak Guide to Shooting Great Travel Pictures* (available at bookstores everywhere) is loaded with tips.

➤ **PHOTO HELP: Kodak Information Center** (tel. 800/242–2424).

EQUIPMENT PRECAUTIONS

Don't pack film and equipment in checked luggage, where it is much more susceptible to damage. X-ray machines used to view checked luggage are becoming much more powerful and therefore are much more likely to ruin your film. Always keep film and tape out of the sun. Carry an extra supply of batteries, and be prepared to turn on your camera or camcorder to prove to security personnel that the device is real. Always ask for hand inspection of film, which becomes clouded after repeated exposure to airport X-ray machines, and keep videotapes away from metal detectors.

Car Rental

All major international car-rental agencies are represented in Copenhagen; most are near the Vesterport Station. Car rentals can begin at $60 a day and $190 a week. This does not include tax on car rentals, which is 25% in Denmark. A service charge is usually added, which ranges from $15–$25.

➤ **MAJOR AGENCIES: Alamo** (tel. 800/522–9696; 020/8759–6200 in the U.K., www.alamo.com). **Avis** (tel. 800/331–1084; 800/879–2847 in Canada; 02/9353–9000 in Australia; 09/525–1982 in New Zealand; 0870/606–0100 in the U.K.; www.avis.com). **Budget** (tel. 800/527–0700; 0870/156–5656 in the U.K.; www.budget.com). **Dollar** (tel. 800/800–6000; 0124/622–0111 in the U.K., where it's affiliated with Sixt; 02/9223–1444 in Australia; www.dollar.com). **Hertz** (tel. 800/654–3001; 800/263–0600 in Canada; 020/8897–2072 in the U.K.; 02/9669–2444 in Australia; 09/256–8690 in New Zealand; www.hertz.com). **National Car Rental** (tel. 800/227–7368; 020/8680–4800 in the U.K.; www.nationalcar.com).

CUTTING COSTS

To get the best deal, **book through a travel agent who will shop around.** Do **look into wholesalers,** companies that do not own fleets but rent in bulk from those that do and often offer better rates than traditional car-rental operations. Payment must be made before you leave home.

➤ **LOCAL AGENCIES: Budget-Pitzner Auto** (Copenhagen Airport, tel. 32/50–90–65). **Europcar** (Copenhagen Airport, tel. 32/50–30–90).

➤ **WHOLESALERS: Auto Europe** (tel. 207/842–2000 or 800/223–5555, fax 207/842–2222, www.autoeurope.com). **Europe by Car** (tel. 212/581–3040 or 800/223–1516, fax 212/246–1458, www.europebycar.com). **DER Travel Services** (9501 W. Devon Ave., Rosemont, IL 60018, tel. 800/782–2424, fax 800/282–7474 for information; 800/860–9944 for brochures, www.dertravel. com).**Kemwel Holiday Autos** (tel. 800/678–0678, fax 914/825–3160, www.kemwel.com).

INSURANCE

When driving a rented car you are generally responsible for any damage to or loss of the vehicle. Before you rent, see what coverage your personal auto-insurance policy and credit cards provide.

Before you buy collision coverage, check your existing policies—you may already be covered. However, collision policies that car-rental companies sell for European rentals usually do not include stolen-vehicle coverage.

REQUIREMENTS & RESTRICTIONS

Ask about age requirements: Several countries require drivers to be over 20 years old, but some car-rental companies require that drivers be at least 25. In Scandinavia your own driver's license is acceptable for a limited time; check with the Denmark tourist board before you go. An International Driver's Permit is a good idea; it's available from the American or Canadian Automobile Association, or, in the United Kingdom, from the Automobile Association or Royal Automobile Club.

SURCHARGES

Before you pick up a car in one city and leave it in another, ask about drop-off charges or one-way service fees, which can be substantial. Note, too, that some rental agencies charge extra if you return the car before the time specified in your contract. To avoid a hefty refueling fee, fill the tank just before you turn in the car, but be aware that gas stations near the rental outlet may overcharge.

Car Travel

The E–20 highway, via bridges, connects Fredericia (on Jylland) with Middelfart (on Fyn), a distance of 16 km (10 mi), and goes on to Copenhagen, another 180 km (120 mi) east. Farther north, from Århus (in Jylland), you can get direct auto-catamaran service to Kalundborg (on Sjælland). From there, Route 23 leads to Roskilde, about 72 km (45 mi) east. Take Route 21 east and follow the signs to Copenhagen, another 40 km (25 mi). Make reservations for the ferry in advance through Mols-Linien. (Note: During the busy summer months, passengers without reservations for their vehicles can wait hours.) Another option is to take the car-ferry hydrofoil between Fyn's Ebeltoft or Århus to Odden on Sjælland; the trip takes about one hour. Since the inauguration of the Øresund Bridge in July 2000, Copenhagen is now linked to Malmö, Sweden. The trip takes about 30 minutes, and the steep bridge toll starts at about Dkr 240 per car.

Also be aware that there are relatively low legal blood-alcohol limits and tough penalties for driving while intoxicated in Scandinavia. Penalties include suspension of the driver's license and fines or imprisonment and are enforced by random police roadblocks in urban areas on weekends. In addition, an accident involving a driver with an illegal blood-alcohol level usually voids all insurance agreements, so the driver becomes responsible for his own medical bills and damage to the cars.

Keep your headlights on at all times; this is required by law in most of Scandinavia. Also by Scandinavian law, everyone, including infants, must wear seat belts.

If you are planning on seeing the sites of central Copenhagen, a car is not convenient. Parking spaces are at a premium and, when available, are expensive. A maze of one-way streets, relatively aggressive drivers, and bicycle lanes make it even more complicated. If you are going to drive, choose a small car that's easy to parallel park, bring a lot of small change to feed the meters, and be very aware of the cyclists on your right-hand side: they always have the right-of-way. For emergencies, contact Falck.

➤ **RESERVATIONS: Mols-Linien** (tel. 70/10–14–18).

AUTO CLUBS
➤ **IN AUSTRALIA: Australian Automobile Association** (tel. 02/6247–7311).

➤ **IN CANADA: Canadian Automobile Association** (CAA, tel. 613/247–0117).

➤ **IN NEW ZEALAND: New Zealand Automobile Association** (tel. 09/377–4660).

➤ **IN THE U.K.: Automobile Association** (AA, tel. 0990/500–600). **Royal Automobile Club** (RAC, tel. 0990/722–722 for membership; 0345/121–345 for insurance).

➤ **IN THE U.S.: American Automobile Association** (tel. 800/564–6222).

EMERGENCY SERVICES
Before leaving home, consult your insurance company. Members of organizations affiliated with Alliance International de Tourisme (AIT) can get technical and legal advice from the Danish Motoring Organization, open 10–4 weekdays. All

highways have emergency phones, and you can call the rental company for help. If you cannot drive your car to a garage for repairs, the rescue corps Falck can help anywhere, anytime. In most cases they do charge for assistance.

➤ **CONTACTS: Auto Rescue/Falck** (tel. 70/10–20–30). **Danish Motoring Organization** (FDM; Firskovvej 32, 2800 Lyngby, tel. 45/27–07–07).

GASOLINE
Gasoline costs about Dkr 8 per liter (¼ gallon).

PARKING
You can usually park on the right-hand side of the road, though not on main roads and highways. Signs reading PARKERING/STANDSNING FORBUNDT mean no parking or stopping, though you are allowed a three-minute grace period for loading and unloading. In town, parking disks are used where there are no automated ticket-vending machines. Get disks from gas stations, post offices, police stations, or tourist offices, and set them to show your time of arrival. For most downtown parking, you must buy a ticket from an automatic vending machine and display it on the dash. Parking costs about Dkr 10 or more per hour.

RULES OF THE ROAD
To drive in Denmark you need a valid driver's license, and if you're using your own car, it must have a certificate of registration and national plates. A triangular hazard-warning sign is compulsory in every car and is provided with rentals. No matter where you sit in a car, you must wear a seat belt, and cars must have low beams on at all times. Motorcyclists must wear helmets and use low-beam lights as well.

Drive on the right and give way to traffic—*especially to bicyclists*—on the right. A red-and-white YIELD sign or a line of white triangles across the road means you must yield to traffic on the road you are entering. Do not turn right on red unless there is a green arrow indicating that this is allowed. Speed limits are 50 kph (30 mph) in built-up areas; 100 kph (60 mph) on highways; and 80 kph (50 mph) on other roads. If you are towing a trailer, you must not exceed 70 kph (40 mph). Speeding and, especially, drinking and driving are treated severely, even if no damage is caused. Americans and other foreign tourists must pay fines on the spot.

Children in Copenhagen

In Denmark, children are to be seen *and* heard and are genuinely welcome in most public places.

If you are renting a car, don't forget to **arrange for a car seat** when you reserve. For general advice about traveling with children, consult *Fodor's FYI: Travel with Your Baby* (available in bookstores everywhere).

DISCOUNTS

Children are entitled to discount tickets (often as much as 50% off) on buses, trains, and ferries throughout Scandinavia, as well as reductions on special City Cards. Children under age 12 pay 75% of the adult fare and children under age 2 pay 10% on SAS round-trips. There are no restrictions on the children's fares when booked in economy class. "Family fares," only available in business class, are also worth looking into (☞ Cutting Costs in Air Travel).

With the Scanrail Pass—good for rail journeys throughout Scandinavia—children under age 4 (on lap) travel free; those ages 4–11 pay half-fare and those ages 12–25 can get a Scanrail Youth Pass, providing a 25% discount off the adult fare.

FLYING

If your children are age 2 or older, **ask about children's airfares.** As a general rule, infants under 2 not occupying a seat fly at greatly reduced fares or even for free. When booking, **confirm carry-on allowances** if you're traveling with infants. In general, for babies charged 10% of the adult fare you are allowed one carry-on bag and a collapsible stroller; if the flight is full, the stroller may have to be checked or you may be limited to less.

Experts agree that it's a good idea to use safety seats aloft for children weighing less than 40 pounds. Airlines set their own policies: U.S. carriers usually require that the child be ticketed, even if he or she is young enough to ride free, since the seats must be strapped into regular seats. Do **check your airline's policy about using safety seats during takeoff and landing.** And since safety seats are not allowed everywhere in the plane, get your seat assignments early.

When reserving, **request children's meals or a freestanding bassinet** if you need them. But note that bulkhead seats, where you must sit to use the bassinet, may lack an overhead bin or storage space on the floor. For all airlines servicing Scandinavia, it is necessary to reserve children's and baby meals at least 24 hours in advance; travel of an unaccompanied minor should be confirmed at least three days prior to the flight.

LODGING

Most hotels in Scandinavia allow children under a certain age to stay in their parents' room at no extra charge, but others charge for them as extra adults; be sure to **find out the cutoff age for children's discounts.**

SIGHTS & ATTRACTIONS

Places that are especially appealing to children are indicated by a rubber-duckie icon (🐥) in the margin.

Consumer Protection

Whenever shopping or buying travel services in Scandinavia, **pay with a major credit card,** if possible, so you can cancel payment or get reimbursed if there's a problem. If you're doing business with a particular company for the first time, contact your local Better Business Bureau and the attorney general's offices in your state and (for U.S. businesses) the company's home state as well. Have any complaints been filed? Finally, if you're buying a package or tour, always consider travel insurance that includes default coverage (☞ Insurance).

➤ **BBBS: Council of Better Business Bureaus** (4200 Wilson Blvd., Suite 800, Arlington, VA 22203, tel. 703/276–0100, fax 703/525–8277, www.bbb.org).

Customs & Duties

When shopping, keep receipts for all purchases. Upon reentering the country, be ready to show customs officials what you've bought. If you feel a duty is incorrect or object to the way your clearance was handled, note the inspector's badge number and ask to see a supervisor. If the problem isn't resolved, write to the appropriate authorities, beginning with the port director at your point of entry.

IN AUSTRALIA
Australian residents who are 18 or older may bring home $A400 worth of souvenirs and gifts (including jewelry), 250 cigarettes or 250 grams of tobacco, and 1,125 ml of alcohol (including wine, beer, and spirits). Residents under 18 may bring back $A200 worth of goods. Prohibited items include meat products. Seeds, plants, and fruits need to be declared upon arrival.

➤ **INFORMATION: Australian Customs Service** (Regional Director, Box 8, Sydney, NSW 2001, Australia, tel. 02/9213–2000, fax 02/9213–4000, www.customs.gov.au).

IN CANADA
Canadian residents who have been out of Canada for at least seven days may bring home C$750 worth of goods duty-free. If

you've been away fewer than seven days but more than 48 hours, the duty-free allowance drops to C$200; if your trip lasts 24–48 hours, the allowance is C$50. You may not pool allowances with family members. Goods claimed under the C$750 exemption may follow you by mail; those claimed under the lesser exemptions must accompany you. Alcohol and tobacco products may be included in the seven-day and 48-hour exemptions but not in the 24-hour exemption. If you meet the age requirements of the province or territory through which you reenter Canada, you may bring in, duty-free, 1.14 liters (40 imperial ounces) of wine or liquor or 24 12-ounce cans or bottles of beer or ale. If you are 19 or older you may bring in, duty-free, 200 cigarettes and 50 cigars. Check ahead of time with the Canada Customs Revenue Agency or the Department of Agriculture for policies regarding meat products, seeds, plants, and fruits.

You may send an unlimited number of gifts worth up to C$60 each duty-free to Canada. Label the package UNSOLICITED GIFT— VALUE UNDER $60. Alcohol and tobacco are excluded.

➤ **INFORMATION: Canada Customs and Revenue Agency** (2265 St. Laurent Blvd. S, Ottawa, Ontario K1G 4K3, Canada, tel. 204/ 983–3500 or 506/636–5064; 800/461–9999 in Canada, www.ccra-adrc.gc.ca).

IN DENMARK

If you are 21 or older, have purchased goods in a country that is a member of the European Union (EU), and pay that country's value-added tax (V.A.T.) on those goods, you may import duty-free 1½ liters of liquor; 300 cigarettes or 150 cigarillos or 75 cigars or 400 grams of tobacco. If you are entering Denmark from a non-EU country or if you have purchased your goods on a ferryboat or in an airport not taxed in the EU, you must pay Danish taxes on any amount of alcoholic beverages greater than 1 liter of liquor or 2 liters of strong wine, plus 2 liters of table wine. For tobacco, the limit is 200 cigarettes or 100 cigarillos or

50 cigars or 250 grams of tobacco. You are also allowed 50 grams of perfume. Other articles (including beer) are allowed up to a maximum of Dkr 1,350.

IN NEW ZEALAND

Homeward-bound residents 17 or older may bring back $700 worth of souvenirs and gifts. Your duty-free allowance also includes 4.5 liters of wine or beer; one 1,125-ml bottle of spirits; and either 200 cigarettes, 250 grams of tobacco, 50 cigars, or a combination of the three up to 250 grams. Prohibited items include meat products, seeds, plants, and fruits.

➤ **INFORMATION: New Zealand Customs** (Custom House, 50 Anzac Ave., Box 29, Auckland, New Zealand, tel. 09/300–5399, fax 09/359–6730, www.customs.govt.nz).

IN THE U.K.

If you are a U.K. resident and your journey was wholly within the European Union (EU), you won't have to pass through customs when you return to the United Kingdom. If you plan to bring back large quantities of alcohol or tobacco, check EU limits beforehand. From countries outside the European Union, including Iceland and Norway, you may bring home, duty-free, 200 cigarettes or 50 cigars; 1 liter of spirits or 2 liters of fortified or sparkling wine or liqueurs; 2 liters of still table wine; 60 ml of perfume; 250 ml of toilet water; plus £145 worth of other goods, including gifts and souvenirs. If returning from outside the EU, prohibited items include meat products, seeds, plants, and fruits.

➤ **INFORMATION: HM Customs and Excise** (St. Christopher House, Southwark, London, SE1 0TE, U.K., tel. 020/7928–3344, www.hmce.gov.uk).

IN THE U.S.

U.S. residents who have been out of the country for at least 48 hours (and who have not used the $400 allowance or any part of it in the past 30 days) may bring home $400 worth of foreign goods duty-free.

U.S. residents age 21 and older may bring back 1 liter of alcohol duty-free. In addition, regardless of your age, you are allowed 200 cigarettes and 100 non-Cuban cigars. Antiques, which the U.S. Customs Service defines as objects more than 100 years old, enter duty-free, as do original works of art done entirely by hand, including paintings, drawings, and sculptures.

You may also mail or ship packages home duty-free: up to $200 worth of goods for personal use, with a limit of one parcel per addressee per day (except alcohol or tobacco products or perfume worth more than $5); label the package PERSONAL USE and attach a list of its contents and their retail value. Do not label the package UNSOLICITED GIFT or your duty-free exemption will drop to $100. Mailed items do not affect your duty-free allowance on your return.

➤ **INFORMATION: U.S. Customs Service** (1300 Pennsylvania Ave. NW, Room 6.3D, Washington, DC 20229, www.customs.gov; inquiries tel. 202/354–1000; complaints c/o 1300 Pennsylvania Ave. NW, Room 5.4D, Washington, DC 20229; registration of equipment c/o Office of Passenger Programs, tel. 202/927–0530).

Dining

Copenhagen offers a full range of dining choices, from traditional to international restaurants. The restaurants we list are the cream of the crop in each price category.

MEALS & SPECIALTIES

The surrounding oceans and plentiful inland lakes and streams provide Scandinavian countries with an abundance of fresh fish and seafood: salmon, herring, trout, and seafood delicacies are mainstays, and are prepared in countless ways. Berries and mushrooms are still harvested from the forests; sausage appears in a thousand forms, as do potatoes and other root vegetables such as turnips, radishes, rutabaga, and carrots. Some particular northern tastes can seem unusual, such as the fondness for pickled and fermented fish—to be sampled carefully at first—and a universal obsession with sweet pastries, ice cream, and chocolate.

MEALTIMES

Unless otherwise noted, the restaurants listed in this guide are open daily for lunch and dinner.

RESERVATIONS & DRESS

Reservations are always a good idea: we mention them only when they're essential or not accepted. Book as far ahead as you can, and reconfirm as soon as you arrive. We mention dress only when men are required to wear a jacket or a jacket and tie.

WINE, BEER & SPIRITS

Restaurants' markup on alcoholic beverages is often very high in Scandinavia: as much as four times that of a standard retail price.

Disabilities & Accessibility

Facilities for travelers with disabilities in Copenhagen are generally good, and most of the major tourist offices offer special booklets and brochures on travel and accommodations. Notify and make all local and public transportation and hotel reservations in advance to ensure a smooth trip.

LODGING

Best Western offers properties with wheelchair-accessible rooms just outside Copenhagen. If wheelchair-accessible rooms on other floors are not available, ground-floor rooms are provided.

➤ **WHEELCHAIR-FRIENDLY CHAIN: Best Western** (tel. 800/528–1234).

RESERVATIONS

When discussing accessibility with an operator or reservations agent, **ask hard questions.** Are there any stairs, inside or out? Are there grab bars next to the toilet *and* in the shower/tub? How wide is the doorway to the room? To the bathroom? For the most extensive facilities, **opt for newer accommodations.**

SIGHTS & ATTRACTIONS

Although most major attractions in Copenhagen present no problems, windy cobblestone streets in the older sections may be challenging for travelers with disabilities.

TRANSPORTATION

With advance notice, most airlines, buses, and trains can arrange assistance for those requiring extra help with boarding. Contact each individual company at least one week in advance, or ideally at the time of booking.

➤ **COMPLAINTS: Aviation Consumer Protection Division** (C-75, Room 4107, Washington, DC 20590, tel. 202/366–2220) for airline-related problems. **Civil Rights Office** (U.S. Department of Transportation, Departmental Office of Civil Rights, S-30, 400 7th St. SW, Room 10215, Washington, DC 20590, tel. 202/366–4648, fax 202/366–9371, www.dot.gov/ost/docr/index.htm) for problems with surface transportation. **Disability Rights Section** (U.S. Department of Justice, Civil Rights Division, Box 66738, Washington, DC 20035-6738, tel. 202/514–0301 or 800/514–0301; 202/514–0383 TTY; 800/514–0383 TTY, fax 202/307–1198, www.usdoj.gov/crt/ada/adahom1.htm) for general complaints.

TRAVEL AGENCIES

In the United States, the Americans with Disabilities Act requires that travel firms serve the needs of all travelers. Some agencies specialize in working with people with disabilities.

➤ **TRAVELERS WITH MOBILITY PROBLEMS: Access Adventures** (206 Chestnut Ridge Rd., Scottsville, NY 14624, tel. 716/889–9096), run by a former physical-rehabilitation counselor. **CareVacations** (No. 5, 5110–50 Ave., Leduc, Alberta T9E 6V4, Canada, tel. 780/986–6404 or 877/478–7827, fax 780/986–8332, www.carevacations.com), for group tours and cruise vacations. **Flying Wheels Travel** (143 W. Bridge St., Box 382, Owatonna, MN 55060, tel. 507/451–5005 or 800/535–6790, fax 507/451–1685, www.flyingwheelstravel.com).

Discounts & Deals

Be a smart shopper and **compare all your options** before making decisions. A plane ticket bought with a promotional coupon from travel clubs, coupon books, and direct-mail offers or on the Internet may not be cheaper than the least expensive fare from a discount ticket agency. And always keep in mind that what you get is just as important as what you save.

DISCOUNT RESERVATIONS

To save money, **look into discount reservations services** with toll-free numbers, which use their buying power to get a better price on hotels, airline tickets, even car rentals. When booking a room, always **call the hotel's local toll-free number** (if one is available) rather than the central reservations number—you'll often get a better price. Always ask about special packages or corporate rates.

When shopping for the best deal on hotels and car rentals, **look for guaranteed exchange rates,** which protect you against a falling dollar. With your rate locked in, you won't pay more, even if the price goes up in the local currency.

➤ **AIRLINE TICKETS: tel. 800/247–4537.**

➤ **HOTEL ROOMS: International Marketing & Travel Concepts** (tel. 800/790–4682, www.imtc-travel.com). **Players Express**

Vacations (tel. 800/458–6161, www.playersexpress.com). **Steigenberger Reservation Service** (tel. 800/223–5652, www.srs-worldhotels.com). **Travel Interlink** (tel. 800/888–5898, www.travelinterlink.com). **Turbotrip.com** (tel. 800/473–7829, www.turbotrip.com).

PACKAGE DEALS

Don't confuse packages and guided tours. When you buy a package, you travel on your own, just as though you had planned the trip yourself. Fly/drive packages, which combine airfare and car rental, are often a good deal. If you **buy a rail/drive pass,** you may save on train tickets and car rentals. All Eurail- and Europass holders get a discount on Eurostar fares through the Channel Tunnel. Also check rates for Scanrail Passes.

Electricity

To use electric-powered equipment purchased in the United States or Canada, **bring a converter and adapter.** The electrical current in Scandinavia is 220 volts, 50 cycles alternating current (AC); wall outlets take Continental-type plugs, with two round prongs.

If your appliances are dual-voltage, you'll need only an adapter. Don't use 110-volt outlets marked FOR SHAVERS ONLY for high-wattage appliances such as blow-dryers. Most laptops operate equally well on 110 and 220 volts and so require only an adapter.

Embassies

New Zealanders should contact the UK embassy for assistance.

➤ **AUSTRALIA: (Strandboulevarden 122, DK–2100 Copenhagen Ø, tel. 70/26–36–76).**

➤ **CANADA: (Kristen Bernikows G. 1, DK–1105 Copenhagen Ø, tel. 33/12–22–99.**

➤ **UNITED KINGDOM:** (Kastesvej 40, DK–2100 Copenhagen Ø, tel. 35/44–52–00).

➤ **UNITED STATES:** (Dag Hammarskjölds Allé 24, DK–2100 Copenhagen Ø, tel. 35/55–31–44).

Emergencies

The general emergency number throughout Denmark is 112. Emergency dentists, near Østerport Station, are available weekdays 8 PM–9:30 PM and weekends and holidays 10 AM–noon. The only acceptable payment method is cash. For emergency doctors, look in the phone book under *læge*. After normal business hours, emergency doctors make house calls in the central city and accept cash only; night fees are approximately Dkr 300–Dkr 400. You can also contact the U.S., Canadian, or British embassies for information on English-speaking doctors.

➤ **DOCTORS AND DENTISTS: Emergency dentists** (14 Oslo Pl.). **Emergency doctors** (tel. 38/88–60–41).

➤ **EMERGENCY SERVICES: Police, fire, and ambulance** (tel. 112).

➤ **HOSPITALS: Frederiksberg Hospital** (Nordre Fasanvej 57, tel. 38/34–77–11). **Rigshospitalet** (Blegdamsvej 9, tel. 35/45–35–45).

➤ **24-HOUR PHARMACIES: Sønderbro Apotek** (Amangerbrog. 158, tel. 32/58–01–40). **Steno Apotek** (Vesterbrog. 6C, tel. 33/14–82–66).

English-Language Media

BOOKS

Boghallen, the bookstore of the Politiken publishing house, offers a good selection of English-language books. Arnold Busck has an excellent selection, and also textbooks, CDs, and comic books.

➤ **BOOKSTORES: Arnold Busck** (Kobmagerg. 49, tel. 33/12–24–53). **Boghallen** (Rådhus Pl. 37, tel. 33/11–85–11 Ext. 309).

NEWSPAPERS AND MAGAZINES

The Copenhagen Post (www.cphpost.dk) is a weekly newspaper that covers Danish news events in English. Particularly helpful is its insert, *In & Out*, with reviews and listings of restaurants, bars, nightclubs, concerts, theater, temporary exhibits, flea markets, and festivals in Copenhagen. Anyone planning on staying in Copenhagen for a long period should peruse the classified ads listing apartment-rental agencies and jobs for English-speakers. It's available at select bookstores, some hotels, and the tourist office. The biannual magazine *Copenhagen Living* (www.cphliving.dk) includes articles on Danish culture, food, and architecture and also lists the latest bars, restaurants, and shops. It's sold at some stores, hotels, and the tourist office.

Gay & Lesbian Travel

Scandinavia has a liberal attitude toward gays and lesbians. The government of Denmark grants to same-sex couples the same or nearly the same rights as those who are married.

Copenhagen has an active, although not large, gay community and nightlife.

➤ **GAY- & LESBIAN-FRIENDLY TRAVEL AGENCIES: Different Roads Travel** (8383 Wilshire Blvd., Suite 902, Beverly Hills, CA 90211, tel. 323/651–5557 or 800/429–8747, fax 323/651–3678). **Kennedy Travel** (314 Jericho Turnpike, Floral Park, NY 11001, tel. 516/352–4888 or 800/237–7433, fax 516/354–8849, www.kennedytravel.com). **Now Voyager** (4406 18th St., San Francisco, CA 94114, tel. 415/626–1169 or 800/255–6951, fax 415/626–8626, www.nowvoyager.com). **Skylink Travel and Tour** (1006 Mendocino Ave., Santa Rosa, CA 95401, tel. 707/546–9888 or 800/225–5759, fax 707/546–9891, www.skylinktravel.com), serving lesbian travelers.

Holidays

In Denmark, the following holidays are celebrated: New Year's Eve and Day; Maundy Thursday, Good Friday, Easter and Easter Monday; First Day of Summer, Apr. 25; Labor Day, May 1; National Day, June 17; Midsummer Eve and Day, June 21; Bank Holiday Monday, Aug. 5; Christmas (as well as Christmas Eve and Boxing Day, the day after Christmas).

On major holidays such as Christmas, most shops close or operate on a Sunday schedule. On the eves of such holidays, many shops are also closed all day or are open with reduced hours.

On May Day, the city centers are usually full of people, celebrations, and parades. During Midsummer, at the end of June, locals flock to the lakes and countryside to celebrate the beginning of long summer days with bonfires and other festivities.

Insurance

The most useful travel-insurance plan is a comprehensive policy that includes coverage for trip cancellation and interruption, default, trip delay, and medical expenses (with a waiver for pre-existing conditions).

Without insurance you will lose all or most of your money if you cancel your trip, regardless of the reason. Default insurance covers you if your tour operator, airline, or cruise line goes out of business. Trip-delay covers expenses that arise because of bad weather or mechanical delays. Study the fine print when comparing policies.

If you're traveling internationally, a key component of travel insurance is coverage for medical bills incurred if you get sick on the road. Such expenses are not generally covered by Medicare or private policies. U.K. residents can buy a travel-insurance policy valid for most vacations taken during the year in which it's purchased (but check pre-existing-condition coverage). British and Australian citizens need extra medical coverage when traveling overseas.

Always buy travel policies directly from the insurance company; if you buy them from a cruise line, airline, or tour operator that goes out of business you probably will not be covered for the agency or operator's default, a major risk. Before making any purchase, review your existing health and homeowner's policies to find what they cover away from home.

➤ TRAVEL INSURERS: In the U.S.: Access America (6600 W. Broad St., Richmond, VA 23230, tel. 800/284–8300, fax 804/673–1491, www.etravelprotection.com). Travel Guard International (1145 Clark St., Stevens Point, WI 54481, tel. 715/345–0505 or 800/826–1300, fax 800/955–8785, www.travelguard.com).

➤ INSURANCE INFORMATION: In the U.K.: Association of British Insurers (51–55 Gresham St., London EC2V 7HQ, U.K., tel. 020/7600–3333, fax 020/7696–8999, www.abi.org.uk). In Canada: RBC Travel Insurance (6880 Financial Dr., Mississauga, Ontario L5N 7Y5, Canada, tel. 905/791–8700; 800/668–4342 in Canada, fax 905/816–2498, www.royalbank.com). In Australia: Insurance Council of Australia (Level 3, 56 Pitt St., Sydney NSW 2000, tel. 02/9253–5100, fax 02/9253–5111, www.ica.com.au). In New Zealand: Insurance Council of New Zealand (Level 7, 111–115 Customhouse Quay, Box 474, Wellington, New Zealand, tel. 04/472–5230, fax 04/473–3011, www.icnz.org.nz).

Language

Most Danes, except those in rural areas, speak English well. English becomes rarer outside major cities, and it's a good idea to take along a dictionary or phrase book. Even here, however, anyone under the age of 50 is likely to have studied English in school.

Lodging

The lodgings we list are the cream of the crop in each price category. We always list the facilities that are available—but we don't specify whether they cost extra: When pricing accommodations, always ask what's included and what costs extra.

Before you leave home, **ask your travel agent about discounts,** including summer hotel checks for Best Western, and Scandic, and enormous year-round rebates at SAS hotels for travelers over 65. All EuroClass (business class) passengers can get discounts of at least 10% at SAS hotels when they book through SAS.

Assume that hotels operate on the **European Plan** (EP, with no meals) unless we specify that they use the **Continental Plan** (CP, with a Continental breakfast), **Modified American Plan** (MAP, with breakfast and dinner), or the **Full American Plan** (FAP, with all meals).

Make reservations whenever possible. Even countryside inns, which usually have space, are sometimes packed with vacationing Europeans.

APARTMENT RENTALS

If you want a home base that's roomy enough for a family and comes with cooking facilities, **consider a furnished rental.** These can save you money, especially if you're traveling with a group. Home-exchange directories sometimes list rentals as well as exchanges.

➤ **INTERNATIONAL AGENTS: Drawbridge to Europe** (98 Granite St., Ashland, OR 97520, tel. 541/482–7778 or 888/268–1148, fax 541/482–7779, www.drawbridgetoeurope.com).

HOME EXCHANGES

If you would like to exchange your home for someone else's, **join a home-exchange organization,** which will send you its updated listings of available exchanges for a year and will include your own listing in at least one of them. It's up to you to make specific arrangements.

➤ **EXCHANGE CLUBS: HomeLink International** (Box 47747, Tampa, FL 33647, tel. 813/975–9825 or 800/638–3841, fax 813/910–8144, www.homelink.org; $106 per year). **Intervac U.S.** (Box 590504, San Francisco, CA 94159, tel. 800/756–4663, fax 415/435–7440, www.intervacus.com; $93 yearly fee includes one catalog and on-line access).

HOSTELS
No matter what your age, you can **save on lodging costs by staying at hostels.** In some 4,500 locations in more than 70 countries around the world, Hostelling International (HI), the umbrella group for a number of national youth-hostel associations, offers single-sex, dorm-style beds and, at many hostels, rooms for couples and family accommodations. Membership in any HI national hostel association, open to travelers of all ages, allows you to stay in HI-affiliated hostels at member rates; one-year membership is about $25 for adults (C$26.75 in Canada, £9.30 in the U.K., $30 in Australia, and $30 in New Zealand); hostels run about $10–$25 per night. If a hostel has nearly filled up, members have priority over others; members are also eligible for discounts around the world, even on rail and bus travel in some countries.

If you have a Hosteling International–American Youth Hostels card (obtainable before you leave home, in Washington, D.C.), the average cost is Dkr 70 to Dkr 85 per person. Without the card, there's a surcharge of Dkr 30. The hostels fill up quickly in summer, so make your reservations early. Most hostels are particularly sympathetic to students and will usually find them at least a place on the floor. Bring your own linens or sleep sheet, though these can usually be rented at the hostel. Sleeping bags are not allowed. Contact Danhostel Danmarks Vandrehjem—it charges for information, but you can get a free brochure,

Camping/Youth and Family Hostels, from the Danish Tourist Board. You can also log on to www.danhostel.com for more information.

➤ **IN COPENHAGEN: Danhostel Danmarks Vandrehjem** (Vesterbrog. 39, DK–1620, Copenhagen V, tel. 33/31–36–12, fax 33/31–36–26).

➤ **ORGANIZATIONS: Hostelling International—American Youth Hostels** (733 15th St. NW, Suite 840, Washington, DC 20005, tel. 202/783–6161, fax 202/783–6171, www.hiayh.org). **Hostelling International—Canada** (400–205 Catherine St., Ottawa, Ontario K2P 1C3, Canada, tel. 613/237–7884; 800/663–5777 in Canada, fax 613/237–7868, www.hostellingintl.ca). **Youth Hostel Association of England and Wales** (Trevelyan House, 8 St. Stephen's Hill, St. Albans, Hertfordshire AL1 2DY, U.K., tel. 0870/8708808, fax 01727/844126, www.yha.org.uk). **Youth Hostel Association Australia** (10 Mallett St., Camperdown, NSW 2050, Australia, tel. 02/9565–1699, fax 02/9565–1325, www.yha.com.au). **Youth Hostels Association of New Zealand** (Level 3, 193 Cashel St., Box 436, Christchurch, New Zealand, tel. 03/379–9970, fax 03/365–4476, www.yha.org.nz).

HOTELS

Many Danes prefer a shower to a bath, so if you particularly want a bath, ask for it, but be prepared to pay more. Taxes are usually included in prices, but check when making a reservation. As time goes on, it appears that an increasing number of hotels are eliminating breakfast from their room rates; even if it is not included, breakfast is usually well worth its price. Many of Denmark's larger hotels, particularly those that cater to the conference crowd, offer discounted rates on the weekends, so inquire when booking.

Try www.danishhotels.dk for hotel listings not included in this book. All hotels listed have private baths unless otherwise noted.

> **TOLL-FREE NUMBERS: Best Western** (tel. 800/528–1234, www.bestwestern.com). **Choice** (tel. 800/221–2222, www.choicehotels.com). **Comfort** (tel. 800/228–5150, www.comfortinn.com). **Hilton** (tel. 800/445–8667, www.hilton.com). **Holiday Inn** (tel. 800/465–4329, www.basshotels.com). **Quality Inn** (tel. 800/228–5151, www.qualityinn.com). **Radisson** (tel. 800/333–3333, www.radisson.com). **Sheraton** (tel. 800/325–3535, www.starwoodhotels.com).

HOUSE RENTALS

A simple house with room for four will cost from Dkr 2,500 per week and up. Contact DanCenter.

> **CONTACTS: DanCenter** (Søtorv 5, DK–1371 Copenhagen, tel. 70/13–00–00).

RESERVING A ROOM

The very friendly staff at the hotel booking desk at Wonderful Copenhagen can help find rooms in hotels, hostels, and private homes in advance of a trip. If you find yourself in Copenhagen without a reservation, head for the tourist office's hotel booking desk, which is open May through August, Monday through Saturday 9–8 and Sunday 10–8; September through April, weekdays 10–4:30 and Saturday 10–1:30. Note that hours of the hotel booking desk can be fickle, and change from year to year depending on staff availability; in the low season, they are often closed on the weekends. Reservations in private homes and hotels must be done two months in advance, but last-minute (as in same-day) hotel rooms booked at the tourist office can save you 50% off the normal price.

> **RESERVATION INFORMATION: Hotel booking desk** (tel. 33/25–38–44) at Wonderful Copenhagen (Gammel Kongevej 1, DK–1610 Copenhagen).

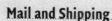
Mail and Shipping

POSTAL RATES

Airmail letters and postcards to the United States cost Dkr 5.50
for 20 grams. Letters and postcards to the United Kingdom and
EU countries cost Dkr 4.50. You can buy stamps at post offices or
from shops selling postcards.

RECEIVING MAIL

You can arrange to have your mail sent general delivery, marked
poste restante, to any post office, hotel, or inn. The address for the
main post office in Copenhagen is Tietgensgade 37, DK–1704
KBH.

Money Matters

Prices throughout this guide are given for adults. Substantially
reduced fees are almost always available for children, students,
and senior citizens.

Denmark's economy is stable, and inflation remains reasonably
low. Although lower than Norway's and Sweden's, the Danish
cost of living is nonetheless high, especially for cigarettes
and alcohol. Some sample prices: cup of coffee, Dkr 18–Dkr 25;
bottle of beer, Dkr 18–Dkr 30; soda, Dkr 10–Dkr 15; ham
sandwich, Dkr 25–Dkr 40; 1-mi taxi ride, Dkr 35–Dkr 50,
depending on traffic.

Sales taxes can be very high, but foreigners can get some
refunds by shopping at tax-free stores.

You can **reduce the cost of food by planning.** Breakfast is often
included in your hotel bill; if not, you may wish to buy fruit,
sweet rolls, and a beverage for a picnic breakfast. Electrical
devices for hot coffee or tea should be bought abroad, though,
to conform to the local current.

Opt for a restaurant lunch instead of dinner, since the latter tends to be significantly more expensive. Instead of beer or wine, **drink tap water**—liquor can cost four times the price of the same brand in a store—but do specify tap water, as the term "water" can refer to soft drinks and bottled water, which are also expensive. In Copenhagen, the tip is included in the cost of your meal.

In most of Scandinavia, liquor and strong beer (over 3% alcohol) can be purchased only in state-owned shops, at very high prices, during weekday business hours, usually 9:30 to 6 and in some areas on Saturday until mid-afternoon. Denmark takes a less restrictive approach, with liquor and beer available in the smallest of grocery stores, open weekdays and Saturday morning—but Danish prices, too, are high. (When you visit friends or relatives in Scandinavia, a bottle of liquor or fine wine bought duty-free on the trip over is often much appreciated.)

ATMS
Copenhagen has many ATMs. They typically accept Visa, MasterCard, and Cirrus cards, and Jyske Bank machines accept PLUS cards.

➤ **ATM LOCATIONS: Cirrus** (tel. 800/424–7787).

CREDIT CARDS
Most major credit cards are accepted in Denmark. Traveler's checks can be exchanged in banks and at many hotels, restaurants, and shops.

Throughout this guide, the following abbreviations are used: **AE,** American Express; **DC,** Diners Club; **MC,** MasterCard; and **V,** Visa.

CURRENCY
The monetary unit in Denmark is the krone (Dkr), divided into 100 øre. At press time (fall 2001), the krone stood at 4.48 to the Australian dollar, 12.4 to the British pound, 4.82 to the Canadian

dollar, 9.45 to the Irish punt, 3.56 to the New Zealand dollar, 1.08 to the South African rand and 8.7 to the U.S. dollar. New 50, 100, 200, 500, and 1,000 kroner notes, featuring such celebrated Danes as author Karen Blixen and physicist Niels Bohr, have been issued over the past few years, and the old notes are being phased out.

CURRENCY EXCHANGE

Almost all banks (including the Danske Bank at the airport) exchange money. Most hotels cash traveler's checks and exchange major foreign currencies, but they charge a substantial fee and give a lower rate. The exception to the rule—if you travel with cash—are the several locations of Forex (including the main train station and close to the Nørreport station). For up to $500, Forex charges only Dkr 20 for the entire transaction. Keep your receipt and it will even change any remaining money you may still have back to dollars for free. For travelers' checks, it charges Dkr 10 per check. Den Danske Bank exchange is open during and after normal banking hours at the main railway station, daily June through August 7 AM–10 PM, and daily September through May, 7 AM–9 PM. American Express, Nyman and Schultz is open weekdays 9–5 and Saturday 9–noon. The Change Group—open April through October daily 10–8, November through March daily 10–6—has several locations in the city center. Tivoli also exchanges money; it is open May through September, daily noon–11 PM.

Although ATM transaction fees may be higher abroad than at home, ATM rates are excellent because they are based on wholesale rates offered only by major banks. You won't do as well at exchange booths in airports or rail and bus stations, in hotels, in restaurants, or in stores. To avoid lines at airport exchange booths, get a bit of local currency before you leave home.

➤ EXCHANGE SERVICES: American Express, Nyman and Schultz (Nørreg. 7A, 3rd floor, tel. 33/12–23–01). The Change Group

(Vesterbrog. 9A; Østerg. 61; Vimmelskaftet 47; Frederiksbergg. 5; tel. 33/93–04–15). **Den Danske Bank** (main train station, tel. 33/12–04–11; airport, tel. 32/46–02–70). **Forex** (main train station, tel. 33/11–22–20; Nørre Voldgade 90, tel. 33/32–81–00). **International Currency Express** (tel. 888/278–6628 for orders, www.foreignmoney.com). **Thomas Cook Currency Services** (tel. 800/287–7362 for telephone orders and retail locations, www.us.thomascook.com). **Tivoli** (Vesterbrog. 3, tel. 33/15–10–01).

TRAVELER'S CHECKS

Do you need traveler's checks? It depends on where you're headed. If you're going to rural areas and small towns, go with cash; traveler's checks are best used in cities. Lost or stolen checks can usually be replaced within 24 hours. To ensure a speedy refund, buy your own traveler's checks—don't let someone else pay for them: irregularities such as this can cause delays. The person who bought the checks should make the call to request a refund.

Outdoors and Sports

FISHING AND ANGLING

Licenses are required for fishing along the coasts; requirements vary from one area to another for fishing in lakes, streams, and the ocean. Licenses generally cost around Dkr 100 and can be purchased from any post office. Remember—it is illegal to fish within 1,650 ft of the mouth of a stream.

Packing

Bring a folding umbrella and a lightweight raincoat, as it is common for the sky to be clear at 9 AM, rainy at 11 AM, and clear again in time for lunch. Pack casual clothes, as Scandinavians tend to dress more casually than their Continental brethren. If you have trouble sleeping when it is light or are sensitive to strong sun, bring an eye mask and dark sunglasses; the sun rises as early as 4 AM in some areas, and the far-northern latitude causes it to slant at angles unseen elsewhere on the globe.

In your carry-on luggage, **pack an extra pair of eyeglasses or contact lenses and enough of any medication** you take to last the entire trip. You may also ask your doctor to write a spare prescription using the drug's generic name, since brand names may vary from country to country. In luggage to be checked, **never pack prescription drugs or valuables.** To avoid customs delays, carry medications in their original packaging. And don't forget to carry with you the addresses of offices that handle refunds of lost traveler's checks. Check *Fodor's How to Pack* (available in bookstores everywhere) for more tips.

CHECKING LUGGAGE

You are allowed one carry-on bag and one personal article, such as a purse or a laptop computer. Make sure that everything you carry aboard will fit under the seat or in the overhead bin. Get to the gate early, so you can board as soon as possible, before the overhead bins fill up.

If you are flying internationally, note that baggage allowances may be determined not by piece but by weight—generally 88 pounds (40 kilograms) in first class, 66 pounds (30 kilograms) in business class, and 44 pounds (20 kilograms) in economy.

Airline liability for baggage is limited to $1,250 per person on flights within the United States. On international flights it amounts to $9.07 per pound or $20 per kilogram for checked baggage (roughly $640 per 70-pound bag) and $400 per passenger for unchecked baggage. You can buy additional coverage at check-in for about $10 per $1,000 of coverage, but it excludes a rather extensive list of items, shown on your airline ticket.

Before departure, **itemize your bags' contents** and their worth, and label the bags with your name, address, and phone number.

(If you use your home address, cover it so potential thieves can't see it readily.) Inside each bag, **pack a copy of your itinerary.** At check-in, **make sure that each bag is correctly tagged** with the destination airport's three-letter code. If your bags arrive damaged or fail to arrive at all, file a written report with the airline before leaving the airport.

Passports & Visas

When traveling internationally, **carry your passport** even if you don't need one (it's always the best form of I.D.) and **make two photocopies of the data page** (one for someone at home and another for you, carried separately from your passport). If you lose your passport, promptly call the nearest embassy or consulate and the local police.

ENTERING DENMARK
All U.S. citizens, even infants, need only a valid passport to enter Denmark for stays of up to three months.

PASSPORT OFFICES
The best time to apply for a passport or to renew is in fall and winter. Before any trip, check your passport's expiration date, and, if necessary, renew it as soon as possible.

➤ **AUSTRALIAN CITIZENS: Australian Passport Office** (tel. 131–232, www.dfat.gov.au/passports).

➤ **CANADIAN CITIZENS: Passport Office** (tel. 819/994–3500; 800/567–6868 in Canada, www.dfait-maeci.gc.ca/passport).

➤ **NEW ZEALAND CITIZENS: New Zealand Passport Office** (tel. 04/494–0700, www.passports.govt.nz).

➤ **U.K. CITIZENS: London Passport Office** (tel. 0870/521–0410, www.ukpa.gov.uk) for fees and documentation requirements and to request an emergency passport.

➤ **U.S. CITIZENS: National Passport Information Center** (tel. 900/225–5674; calls are 35¢ per minute for automated service, $1.05 per minute for operator service; www.travel.state.gov/npicinfo.html).

Senior-Citizen Travel

To qualify for age-related discounts, **mention your senior-citizen status up front** when booking hotel reservations (not when checking out) and before you're seated in restaurants (not when paying the bill). When renting a car, ask about promotional car-rental discounts, which can be cheaper than senior-citizen rates.

TRAIN TRAVEL

Seniors over 60 are entitled to discount tickets (often as much as 50% off) on buses, trains, and ferries throughout Scandinavia, as well as reductions on special City Cards. Eurail offers discounts on Scanrail and Eurail train passes.

➤ **EDUCATIONAL PROGRAMS: Elderhostel** (11 Ave. de Lafayette, Boston, MA 02111-1746, tel. 877/426–8056, fax 877/426–2166, www.elderhostel.org).

Shopping

Prices in Denmark are never low, but quality is high, and specialties are sometimes less expensive here than elsewhere. Scandinavian design in both furniture and glassware is world-renowned. Danish Lego blocks and furniture are just a few of the items to look for. Keep an eye out for sales, called *udsalg* in Danish.

Sightseeing Tours

The Copenhagen Tourist Board monitors all tours and has brochures and information. Most tours run through the summer until September.

BIKE TOURS

BikeDenmark offers two different self-guided city cycling tours. Choose between the three- to four-hour Copenhagen Tour, which includes the exteriors of the "musts" of the city, including *The Little Mermaid* and Amalienborg. The second is the eight- to nine-hour Dragør Tour, during which you leave the city and bike to the old-fashioned fishing hamlet near Copenhagen. There, you can swim at the beach and explore the ancient heart of the former Dutch colony. The tour package includes maps and a detailed route description. The rental price of the bike, which is available from Københavns Cycle, is an additional Dkr 50 per bike.

➤ **FEES, CONTACTS, AND SCHEDULES: BikeDenmark** (Åboulevarden 1, tel. 35/36–41–00). **Københavns Cycler** (Reventlowsg. 11, tel. 33/33–86–13).

BOAT TOURS

The Harbor and Canal Tour (one hour) leaves from Gammel Strand and the east side of Kongens Nytorv from May to mid-September. Contact Canal Tours or the tourist board for times and rates. The City and Harbor Tour (2¼ hours) includes a short bus trip through town and sails from the Fish Market on Holmens Canal through several more waterways, ending near Strøget. Just south of the embarkation point for the City and Harbor Tour is the equally charming Netto Boats, which also offers hour-long tours for about half the price of its competitors.

➤ **FEES, CONTACTS, AND SCHEDULES: Canal Tours** (tel. 33/13–31–05). **Netto Boats** (tel. 32/54–41–02).

BUS TOURS

The Grand Tour of Copenhagen (2½ hours) includes Tivoli, the New Carlsberg Museum, Christiansborg Castle, Stock Exchange, Danish Royal Theater, Nyhavn, Amalienborg Castle, Gefion Fountain, Grundtvig Church, and Rosenborg Castle. The City Tour (1¼ hours) is more general, passing the New Carlsberg

Museum, Christiansborg Castle, Thorvaldsen Museum, National Museum, Stock Exchange, Danish Royal Theater, Rosenborg Castle, National Art Gallery, Botanical Gardens, Amalienborg Castle, Gefion Fountain, and The Little Mermaid. The Open Top Tours (about 1 hour), which are given on London-style double-decker buses, include stops at Amalienborg, Stock Exchange, Christiansborg, The Little Mermaid, Louis Tussaud's Wax Museum, the National Museum, Ny Carlsberg Glyptotek, Nyhavn, Thorvaldsen Museum, and Tivoli, and give attendees the option to disembark and embark on a later bus. Only the Grand Tour of Copenhagen, which covers the exteriors of the major sites, and the Open Top Tour, which covers less ground but more quickly, are year-round. It's always a good idea to call first to confirm availability. For tour information call Copenhagen Excursions.

➤ FEES AND SCHEDULES: Copenhagen Excursions (tel. 32/54–06–06).

SPECIAL-INTEREST TOURS
You can tour the Royal Porcelain Factory then shop at its store weekdays at 9, 10, and 11 from mid-September through April, and weekdays at 9, 10, 11, 1, and 2 from May to mid-September.

➤ FEES AND SCHEDULES: Royal Porcelain Factory (Smalleg. 45, tel. 38/86–48–59).

WALKING TOURS
Walking tours begin in front of the Tourist Information Office at 10:30 Monday through Saturday from May to September, and take approximately two hours (call to confirm). There are three different routes: uptown on Monday and Thursday, crosstown on Tuesday and Friday, and downtown on Saturday. The American Richard Karpen, who has been living in Denmark for 14 years, offers information on both the interiors and exteriors of buildings and gives insight into the lifestyles, society, and politics of the Danes. A tour of Rosenborg Castle, including the

treasury, is at 1:30 Monday through Thursday from May to September.

➤ **FEES AND SCHEDULES: Tourist Information Office** (Bernstorffsg. 1, tel. 33/11–13–25; 32/97–14–40 to confirm).

Students in Scandinavia

➤ **I.D.S & SERVICES: Council Travel** (CIEE; 205 E. 42nd St., 15th floor, New York, NY 10017, tel. 212/822–2700 or 888/268–6245, fax 212/822–2699, www.councilexchanges.org) for mail orders only, in the United States. **Travel Cuts** (187 College St., Toronto, Ontario M5T 1P7, Canada, tel. 416/979–2406; 800/667–2887 in Canada, fax 416/979–8167, www.travelcuts.com).

Taxes

VALUE-ADDED TAX

All hotel, restaurant, and departure taxes and V.A.T. (what the Danes call *moms*) are automatically included in prices. V.A.T. is 25%; in Denmark, non-EU citizens can obtain a refund of about 13% to 19%. The shops that participate in the tax-free scheme have a white TAX FREE sticker on their windows. Purchases must be at least Dkr 300 per store and must be sealed and unused in Denmark. At the shop, you'll be asked to fill out a form and show your passport. The form can then be turned in at any airport or ferry customs desk, where you can choose a cash or charge-card credit. Keep all your receipts and tags; occasionally, customs authorities do ask to see purchases, so pack them where they will be accessible.

You can claim a V.A.T refund when you leave the last EU country visited; the V.A.T. refund can be obtained in cash from a special office at the airport, or, upon arriving home, you can send your receipts to an office in the country of purchase to receive your refund by mail. Citizens of EU countries are not eligible for the refund.

Note: Tax-free sales of alcohol, cigarettes, and other luxury goods has been abolished among EU countries. Finland's Åland Islands have some special rights under the EU and therefore allow tax-free sales for ferries in transit through its ports. Air travel to the Scandinavia EU member states (Sweden, Finland, Denmark), as well as Norway, no longer allows tax-free sales.

Global Refund is a V.A.T. refund service that makes getting your money back hassle-free. The service is available Europe-wide at 130,000 affiliated stores. In participating stores, **ask for the Global Refund form** (called a Shopping Cheque). Have it stamped like any customs form by customs officials when you leave the European Union (be ready to show customs officials what you've bought). Then take the form to one of the more than 700 Global Refund counters—conveniently located at every major airport and border crossing—and your money will be refunded on the spot in the form of cash, check, or a refund to your credit-card account (minus a small percentage for processing).

➤ **V.A.T. REFUNDS: Global Refund** (99 Main St., Suite 307, Nyack, NY 10960, tel. 800/566–9828, fax 845/348–1549, www.globalrefund.com).

Taxis

The shiny computer-metered Mercedes and Volvo cabs are not cheap. The base charge is Dkr 15, plus Dkr 8–Dkr 10 per km. A cab is available when it displays the sign FRI (free); it can be hailed or picked up in front of the main train station or at taxi stands, or by calling the number below. Outside the city center, always call for a cab, as your attempts to hail one will be in vain. Try Kobenhavns or Amager/Øbro Taxi. Surcharges apply if you order a cab at night.

➤ **TAXI COMPANIES: Kobenhavns Taxa** (tel. 35/35–35–35). **Amager/Øbro Taxi** (tel. 32/51–51–51).

Telephones

Telephone exchanges throughout Denmark were changed over the past couple of years. If you hear a recorded message or three loud beeps, chances are the number you are trying to reach has been changed. KTAS information can always find current numbers.

AREA & COUNTRY CODES

The country code for Denmark is 45.

DIRECTORY AND OPERATOR ASSISTANCE

Most operators speak English. For national directory assistance, dial 118; for an international KTAS operator, dial 113; for a directory-assisted international call, dial 115. You can reach U.S. operators by dialing local access codes.

INTERNATIONAL CALLS

Dial 00, then the country code (1 for the United States and Canada, 44 for Great Britain), the area code, and the number. It's very expensive to telephone or fax from hotels, although the regional phone companies offer a discount after 7:30 PM. It's more economical to make calls from either the Copenhagen main rail station or the airports.

LOCAL CALLS

Phones accept 1-, 2-, 5-, 10-, and 20-kroner coins. Pick up the receiver, dial the number, always including the area code, and wait until the party answers; then deposit the coins. You have roughly a minute per krone; on some phones you can make another call on the same payment if your time has not run out. When it does, you will hear a beep and your call will be disconnected unless you deposit another coin. Dial the eight-digit number for calls anywhere within the country. For calls to the Faroe Islands (298) and Greenland (299), dial 00, then the three-digit code, then the five-digit number. It is often more economical and less frustrating, however, to buy a phone card from a kiosk; coin-operated phones are becoming increasingly rare.

LONG-DISTANCE SERVICES

AT&T, MCI, and Sprint access codes make calling long distance relatively convenient, but you may find the local access number blocked in many hotel rooms. First ask the hotel operator to connect you. If the hotel operator balks, ask for an international operator, or dial the international operator yourself. One way to improve your odds of getting connected to your long-distance carrier is to travel with more than one company's calling card (a hotel may block Sprint, for example, but not MCI). If all else fails, call from a pay phone.

➤ **ACCESS CODES: AT&T USADirect** (tel. 800/10010). **MCI WorldPhone** (tel. 800/10022). **Sprint Global One** (tel. 800/10877).

MOBILE PHONES

Scandinavia has been one of the world leaders in mobile phone development; almost 90% of the population in Scandinavia owns a mobile phone. Although standard North American cellular phones will not work in Scandinavia, Copenhagen has several companies that rent cellular phones to tourists. Contact the local tourist office for details.

Time

Denmark is one hour ahead of Greenwich Mean Time (GMT) and six hours ahead of Eastern Standard Time (EST).

Tipping

The egalitarian Danes do not expect to be tipped. Service is included in bills for hotels, bars, and restaurants. Taxi drivers round up the fare to the next krone but expect no tip. The exception is hotel porters, who receive about Dkr 5 per bag.

Tours & Packages

Because everything is prearranged on a prepackaged tour or independent vacation, you spend less time planning—and often get it all at a good price.

BOOKING WITH AN AGENT

Travel agents are excellent resources. But it's a good idea to collect brochures from several agencies as some agents' suggestions may be influenced by relationships with tour and package firms that reward them for volume sales. If you have a special interest, **find an agent with expertise in that area**; the American Society of Travel Agents has a database of specialists worldwide.

Make sure your travel agent knows the accommodations and other services of the place being recommended. Ask about the hotel's location, room size, beds, and whether it has a pool, room service, or programs for children, if you care about these. Has your agent been there in person or sent others whom you can contact?

Do some homework on your own, too: local tourism boards can provide information about lesser-known and small-niche operators, some of which may sell only direct.

> **TOUR-OPERATOR RECOMMENDATIONS: American Society of Travel Agents** (☞ Travel Agencies). **National Tour Association** (NTA; 546 E. Main St., Lexington, KY 40508, tel. 859/226–4444 or 800/682–8886, www.ntaonline.com). **United States Tour Operators Association** (USTOA; 342 Madison Ave., Suite 1522, New York, NY 10173, tel. 212/599–6599 or 800/468–7862, fax 212/599–6744, www.ustoa.com).

BUYER BEWARE

Each year consumers are stranded or lose their money when tour operators—even large ones with excellent reputations—go out of business. So **check out the operator**. Ask several travel agents about its reputation, and try to **book with a company that has a consumer-protection program.** (Look for information in the company's brochure.) In the United States, members of the National Tour Association and the United States Tour Operators Association are required to set aside funds to cover your payments and travel arrangements in the event that the company defaults. It's also a good idea to choose a company that participates in the American Society of Travel Agents' Tour Operator Program (TOP); ASTA will act as mediator in any disputes between you and your tour operator.

Remember that the more your package or tour includes the better you can predict the ultimate cost of your vacation. Make sure you know exactly what is covered, and **beware of hidden costs.** Are taxes, tips, and transfers included? Entertainment and excursions? These can add up.

Train Travel

Copenhagen's Hovedbanegården (Central Station) is the hub of the DSB network and is connected to most major cities in Europe. Intercity trains leave every hour, usually on the hour, from 6 AM to 10 PM for principal towns in Fyn and Jylland. To find out more, contact the DSB. You can make reservations at the central station, at most other stations, and through travel agents.

Consider a Scanrail Pass, available for travel in Denmark, Sweden, Norway, and Finland for both first- and second-class train travel: you may have five days of unlimited travel in any two-month period ($276 first-class/$204 second-class); 10 days of unlimited travel in two months ($420/$310); or 21 days of consecutive day unlimited train travel ($486/$360). With the Scanrail Pass, you also enjoy travel bonuses, including free or discounted ferry, boat, and bus travel and a Hotel Discount Card that allows 10%–30% off rates for select hotels June–August.

Passengers ages 12–25 can buy **Scanrail Youth Passes** ($207 first-class/$153 second-class, five travel days in two months; $315/$233 for 10 travel days in two months; $365/$270 for 21 days of unlimited travel).

Those over age 60 can **take advantage of the Scanrail Senior Pass,** which offers the travel bonuses of the Scanrail Pass and discounted travel ($246 first-class/$182 second-class, five days; $374/$276 10 days; $432/$321 for 21 consecutive days). Buy Scanrail passes through Rail Europe and travel agents.

For car and train travel, price the Scanrail'n Drive Pass: in 15 days you can get five days of unlimited train travel and two days of car rental (choice of three car categories) with unlimited mileage in Denmark, Norway, and Sweden. You can purchase extra car rental days and choose from first- or second-class train travel. Individual rates for two adults traveling together (compact car $349 first-class/$279 second-class) are considerably lower (about 25%) than for single adults; the third or fourth person sharing the car only needs to purchase a Scanrail pass.

In Scandinavia, you can **use EurailPasses,** which provide unlimited first-class rail travel, in all of the participating countries, for the duration of the pass. If you plan to rack up the miles, get a standard pass. These are available for 15 days ($554), 21 days ($718), one month ($890), two months ($1,260), and three months ($1,558). Eurail- and EuroPasses are available through travel agents and Rail Europe.

If you are an adult traveling with a youth under age 26 and/or a senior, consider buying a **EurailSaver Pass;** this entitles you to second-class train travel at the discount youth or senior fare, provided that you are traveling with the youth or senior at all times. A Saver pass is available for $470 (15 days), $610 (21 days), and $756 (one month); two and three month fares are also available.

In addition to standard EurailPasses, **ask about special rail-pass plans.** Among these are the Eurail YouthPass (for those under age 26), a Eurail FlexiPass (which allows a certain number of travel days within a set period), the Euraildrive Pass, and the EuroPass Drive (which combines travel by train and rental car).

Whichever pass you choose, remember that you must **purchase your pass before you leave** for Europe.

Many travelers assume that rail passes guarantee them seats on the trains they wish to ride. Not so. You need to **book seats ahead even if you are using a rail pass;** seat reservations are required on some European trains, particularly high-speed trains, and are a good idea on trains that may be crowded—particularly in summer on popular routes. You will also need a reservation if you purchase sleeping accommodations.

➤ **WHERE TO BUY RAIL PASSES: CIT Tours Corp.** (342 Madison Ave., Suite 207, New York, NY 10173, tel. 212/697–2100; 800/248–8687; 800/248–7245 in western U.S., www.cit-tours.com). **DER Travel Services** (Box 1606, Des Plaines, IL 60017, tel. 800/782–2424, fax 800/282–7474, www.dertravel.com). **Rail Europe** (226–230 Westchester Ave., White Plains, NY 10604, tel. 800/438–7245, 914/682–5172, or 416/602–4195; 2087 Dundas E, Suite 105, Mississauga, Ontario L4X 1M2, tel. 800/438–7245, 914/682–5172, or 416/602–4195, www.raileurope.com).

➤ **TRAIN INFORMATION: DSB** (tel. 70/13–14–15). **Hovedbanegården** (Vesterbrog., tel. 33/14–17–01).

Transportation around Copenhagen

Copenhagen is small, with most sights within its 1-square-mi center. Wear comfortable shoes and explore it on foot. Or follow the example of the Danes and rent a bike. For those with aching feet, an efficient transit system is available.

The Copenhagen Card offers unlimited travel on buses and suburban trains (S-trains), admission to more than 60 museums and sites around Sjælland, and a reduction on the ferry crossing to Sweden. You can buy the card, which costs Dkr 175 (24 hours), Dkr 295 (48 hours), or Dkr 395 (72 hours) and is half-price for children, at tourist offices and hotels and from travel agents.

Trains and buses operate from 5 AM (Sunday 6 AM) to midnight. After that, night buses run every half hour from 1 AM to 4:30 AM from the main bus station at Rådhus Pladsen to most areas of the city and surroundings. Trains and buses operate on the same ticket system and divide Copenhagen and surrounding areas into three zones. Tickets are validated on a time basis: on the basic ticket, which costs about Dkr 11 per hour, you can travel anywhere in the zone in which you started. A discount klip kort (clip card), good for 10 rides, costs Dkr 85 and must be stamped in the automatic ticket machines on buses or at stations. (If you don't stamp your clip card, you can be fined up to Dkr 500.) Get zone details for S-trains on the information line. The buses have a Danish information line with an automatic answering menu that is not very helpful, but try pressing the number one on your phone and wait for a human to pick up. The phone information line operates daily 7 AM–9:30 PM. You might do better by asking a bus driver or stopping by the HT Buses main office (open weekdays 9–7, Saturday 9–3) on the Rådhus Pladsen, where the helpful staff is organized and speaks enough English to adequately explain bus routes and schedules to tourists.

The latest addition to Copenhagen's public transit system is also one of its most pleasant. The HT harbor buses are ferries that travel up and down the canal, embarking from outside the Royal Library's Black Diamond, with stops at Knippelsbro, Nyhavn, and Holmen, and then back again, with lovely vistas along the way. The harbor buses run six times an hour, daily from 6 AM to 6:25 PM, and tickets cost Dkr 24. If you have a klip kort, you can use it for a trip on the harbor bus.

A metro system was scheduled to be launched sometime in late 2002, will complement the already existing S-trains and is to travel from the western suburbs of Copenhagen to the center, with stops in Frederiksberg, Nørreport, Kongens Nytorv, Christianshavn, and then continue on to Amager.

➤ **CONTACTS: DSB S-train information line** (tel. 33/14–17–01). **HT Buses Main Office and Information Line** (Rådhus Pl. 7, tel. 33/13–14–15).

Travel Agencies

A good travel agent puts your needs first. Look for an agency that has been in business at least five years, emphasizes customer service, and has someone on staff who specializes in your destination. In addition, **make sure the agency belongs to a professional trade organization.** The American Society of Travel Agents (ASTA)—the largest and most influential in the field with more than 26,000 members in some 170 countries—maintains and enforces a strict code of ethics and will step in to help mediate any agent-client dispute if necessary. ASTA (whose motto is "Without a travel agent, you're on your own") also maintains a Web site that includes a directory of agents. (If a travel agency is also acting as your tour operator, *see* Buyer Beware *in* Tours & Packages).

For student and budget travel, try Kilroy Travels Denmark. For charter packages, stick with Spies. Star Tours also handles packages.

➤ **LOCAL AGENT REFERRALS: American Society of Travel Agents** (ASTA; 1101 King St., Suite 200, Alexandria, VA 22314, tel. 800/965–2782 24-hr hot line, fax 703/739–7642, www.astanet.com). **Association of British Travel Agents** (68–71 Newman St., London W1T 3AH, U.K., tel. 020/7637–2444, fax 020/7637–0713, www.abtanet.com). **Association of Canadian Travel Agents** (130 Albert St., Suite 1705, Ottawa, Ontario K1P 5G4, Canada, tel. 613/237–

3657, fax 613/237–7052, www.acta.net). **Australian Federation of Travel Agents** (Level 3, 309 Pitt St., Sydney NSW 2000, Australia, tel. 02/9264–3299, fax 02/9264–1085, www.afta.com.au). **Travel Agents' Association of New Zealand** (Level 5, Paxus House, 79 Boulcott St., Box 1888, Wellington 10033, New Zealand, tel. 04/499–0104, fax 04/499–0827, www.taanz.org.nz).

➤ **IN COPENHAGEN: American Express, Nyman and Schultz** (Nørreg. 7A, tel. 33/12–23–01). **Carlson Wagonslit** (Bredg. 65, tel. 33/63–77–77). **DSB Travel Bureau** (Copenhagen Main Train Station, tel. 33/14–11–26). **Kilroy Travels Denmark** (Skinderg. 28, tel. 33/11–00–44). **Spies** (Nyropsg. 41, tel. 70/10–42–00). **Star Tours** (H. C. Andersens Blvd. 12, tel. 33/11–88–88).

Visitor Information

Wonderful Copenhagen Tourist Information is open May through the first two weeks of September, daily 9–8; the rest of September through April, weekdays 9–4:30 and Saturday 9–1:30. Note that the tourist office hours vary slightly from year to year, so you may want to call ahead. Its well-maintained Web site includes extensive listings of sights and events. Youth information in Copenhagen is available from Use It. Listings and reviews of Copenhagen's museums (including temporary exhibits), sights, and shops are included on www.aok.dk. The Danish Tourist Board's Web site, www.dt.dk, has listings on hotels, restaurants, and sights in Copenhagen and around Denmark.

➤ **TOURIST INFORMATION: Use It** (Rådhusstr. 13, tel. 33/73–06–20). **Wonderful Copenhagen Tourist Information** (Bernstorffsg. 1, DK–1577 Copenhagen V, tel. 33/11–13–25, www.woco.dk).

➤ **U.S. GOVERNMENT ADVISORIES: U.S. Department of State** (Overseas Citizens Services Office, Room 4811 N.S., 2201 C St. NW, Washington, DC 20520, tel. 202/647–5225 for interactive hot line, travel.state.gov/travel/html); enclose a self-addressed, stamped, business-size envelope.

Web Sites

Do check out the World Wide Web when planning your trip. You'll find everything from weather forecasts to virtual tours of famous cities. Be sure to visit Fodors.com (www.fodors.com), a complete travel-planning site. You can research prices and book plane tickets, hotel rooms, rental cars, vacation packages, and more. In addition, you can post your pressing questions in the Travel Talk section. Other planning tools include a currency converter and weather reports, and there are loads of links to travel resources.

When to Go

The Danish tourist season peaks in June, July, and August, when daytime temperatures are often in the 70s (21°C to 26°C) and sometimes rise into the 80s (27°C to 32°C). In general, the weather is not overly warm, and a brisk breeze and brief rainstorms are possible anytime. Nights can be chilly, even in summer.

Visit in summer if you want to experience the delightfully long summer days. In June, the sun rises in Copenhagen at 4 AM and sets at 11 PM. Many attractions extend their hours during the summer, and many shut down altogether when summer ends. Fall, spring, and even winter are pleasant, despite the area's reputation for gloom. The days become shorter quickly, but the sun casts a golden light not seen farther south. On dark days, fires and candlelight will warm you indoors.

The Gulf Stream warms Denmark, making winters there similar to those in London.

CLIMATE

Below are average daily maximum and minimum temperatures for Copenhagen.

➤ **FORECASTS: Weather Channel Connection** (tel. 900/932–8437), 95¢ per minute from a Touch-Tone phone.

COPENHAGEN

Jan.	36F	2C	May	61F	16C	Sept.	64F	18C
	28	− 2		46	8		52	11
Feb.	36F	2C	June	66F	19C	Oct.	54F	12C
	27	− 3		52	11		45	7
Mar.	41F	5C	July	72F	22C	Nov.	45F	7C
	30	− 1		57	14		37	3
Apr.	52F	11C	Aug.	70F	21C	Dec.	39F	4C
	37	3		57	14		34	1

FESTIVALS & SEASONAL EVENTS

➤ **MAR.:** In Copenhagen, Denmark's—and the world's—oldest amusement park, **Bakken,** opens with much fanfare and a motorcycle parade through the city.

➤ **APR.–OCT.: Legoland,** a park constructed of 45 million Lego blocks, is open in Billund, Jylland.

➤ **APR. 16: The Queen's Birthday** is celebrated with the royal guard in full ceremonial dress as the royal family appears before the public on the balcony of Amalienborg.

➤ **MID-APR.–SEPT.: Tivoli** in Copenhagen twinkles with rides, concerts, and entertainment.

➤ **MAY: The Copenhagen Carnival** includes boat parades in Nyhavn and costumed revelers in the streets.

➤ **JUNE: The Viking Festival** in Frederikssund, northwest of Copenhagen, includes open-air performances of a Viking play.

Your checklist for a perfect journey

WAY AHEAD
- Devise a trip budget.
- Write down the five things you want most from this trip. Keep this list handy before and during your trip.
- Make plane or train reservations. Book lodging and rental cars.
- Arrange for pet care.
- Check your passport. Apply for a new one if necessary.
- Photocopy important documents and store in a safe place.

A MONTH BEFORE
- Make restaurant reservations and buy theater and concert tickets. Visit fodors.com for links to local events.
- Familiarize yourself with the local language or lingo.

TWO WEEKS BEFORE
- Replenish your supply of medications.
- Create your itinerary.
- Enjoy a book or movie set in your destination to get you in the mood.

- Develop a packing list. Shop for missing essentials. Repair and launder or dry-clean your clothes.

A WEEK BEFORE
- Stop newspaper deliveries. Pay bills.
- Acquire traveler's checks.
- Stock up on film.
- Label your luggage.
- Finalize your packing list— take less than you think you need.
- Create a toiletries kit filled with travel-size essentials.
- Get lots of sleep. Don't get sick before your trip.

A DAY BEFORE
- Drink plenty of water.
- Check your travel documents.
- Get packing!

DURING YOUR TRIP
- Keep a journal/scrapbook.
- Spend time with locals.
- Take time to explore. Don't plan too much.

On **Midsummer's Night,** Danes celebrate the longest day of the year with bonfires and picnics.

➤ **JUNE–JULY: The Roskilde Festival,** the largest rock concert in northern Europe, attracts dozens of bands and more than 75,000 fans.

➤ **JULY: The Copenhagen Jazz Festival** gathers international and Scandinavian jazz greats for a week of concerts, many of them free.

➤ **NOV.–DEC.: Tivoli Gardens features its annual Christmas Market,** with lots of decorations, gift ideas, and seasonal treats.

➤ **DEC. 24:** If there's a time when Denmark is at its most *hygellig* (roughly translated, warm and cozy), it's during Christmas, a holiday that the Danes celebrate in great style. For Danes, it's Christmas Eve that's the main day. They dance around the tree while singing carols, and then feast on roast duck or goose with *ris à l'amande* (almond rice pudding) for dessert; an almond is hidden inside the pudding and whoever finds it receives a gift.

➤ **NEW YEAR'S EVE: Fireworks** at the Town Hall Square are set off by local revelers.

DANISH VOCABULARY

English	Danish	Pronunciation
BASICS		
Yes/no	Ja/nej	yah/nie
Thank you	Tak	tak
You're welcome	Selv tak	**sell** tak
Excuse me (to apologize)	Undskyld	**unsk**-ul
Hello	Hej	hi
Goodbye	Farvel	fa-**vel**
Today	I dag	ee **day**
Tomorrow	I morgen	ee **morn**
Yesterday	I går	ee **gore**
Morning	Morgen	**more**-n
Afternoon	Eftermiddag	**ef-tah**-mid-day
Night	Nat	nat

NUMBERS		
1	een/eet	een/eet
2	to	toe
3	tre	treh
4	fire	fear
5	fem	fem
6	seks	sex
7	syv	syoo
8	otte	**oh**-te
9	ni	nee
10	ti	tee

DAYS OF THE WEEK

Monday	mandag	man-day
Tuesday	tirsdag	**tears**-day
Wednesday	onsdag	**ons**-day
Thursday	torsdag	**trs**-day
Friday	fredag	**free**-day
Saturday	lørdag	**lore**-day
Sunday	søndag	**soo**(n)-day

USEFUL PHRASES

Do you speak English?	Taler du engelsk?	te-ler doo in-galsk
I don't speak Danish.	Jeg taler ikke Dansk.	yi tal-ler **ick** Dansk
I don't understand.	Jeg forstår ikke.	yi fahr-store **ick**
I don't know.	Det ved jeg ikke.	deh **ved** yi ick
I am American/British.	Jeg er amerikansk/ britisk.	yi ehr a-mehr-i-**kansk**/ bri-tisk
I am sick.	Jeg er syg.	yi ehr **syoo**
Please call a doctor.	Kan du ringe til en læge?	can **doo** rin-geh til en lay-eh
Do you have a vacant room?	Har du et værelse?	har **doo** eet va(l)r-sa
How much does it cost?	Hvad koster det?	va cos-ta **deh**
It's too expensive.	Det er for dyrt.	deh ehr **fohr** dyrt
Beautiful	Smukt	smukt
Help!	Hjælp	yelp
Stop!	Stop	stop
How do I get to . . .	Hvordan kommer jeg til . . .	vore-**dan** kom-mer yi til

. . . the train station?	banegarden	**ban** eh-gore-en
. . . the post office?	postkontoret	**post**-kon-toh-raht
. . . the tourist office?	turistkonoret	too-**reest**-kon-tor-et
. . . the hospital?	hospitalet	hos-peet-**tal**-et
Does this bus go to . . . ?	Går denne bus til . . . ?	**goh** den-na boos til
Where is the W.C.?	Hvor er toilettet?	vor **ehr** toi-le(tt)-et
On the left	Til venstre	til **ven**-strah
On the right	Till højre	til **hoy**-ah
Straight ahead	Lige ud	**lee** u(l)

DINING OUT

Please bring me . . .	Må jeg få . . .	mo yi foh
menu	menu	me-**nu**
fork	gaffel	gaf-**fel**
knife	kniv	kan-**ew**
spoon	ske	skee
napkin	serviet	serv-**eet**
bread	brød	brood
butter	smør	smoor
milk	mælk	malk
pepper	peber	**pee**-wer
salt	salt	selt
sugar	sukker	**su**-kar
water/bottled water	vand/Dansk vand	van/dansk van
The check, please.	Må jeg bede om regningen.	mo yi bi(d) om **ri**-ning

index

166

FODOR'S POCKET COPENHAGEN

EDITORS: Nuha Ansari, John D. Rambow

Editorial Contributors: Catherine Belonogoff, Satu Hummasti, AnneLise Sørensen, Helayne Schiff, Chris Swiac

Editorial Production: Ira-Neil Dittersdorf

Maps: David Lindroth, *cartographer*; Bob Blake and Rebecca Baer, *map editors*

Design: Fabrizio La Rocca, *creative director*; Tigist Getachew, *art director*; Melanie Marin, *photo editor*

Production/Manufacturing: Yexenia (Jessie) Markland

Cover Photograph: Tina Buckman/Index Stock (Grabodrctery Square)

First Edition

ISBN 1–4000–1163–9

ISSN 1538–7593

IMPORTANT TIP

Although all prices, opening times, and other details in this book are based on information supplied to us at press time, changes occur all the time in the travel world, and Fodor's cannot accept responsibility for facts that become outdated or for inadvertent errors or omissions. So always confirm information when it matters, especially if you're making a detour to visit a specific place.

SPECIAL SALES

Fodor's Travel Publications are available at special discounts for bulk purchases for sales promotions or premiums. Special editions, including personalized covers, excerpts of existing guides, and corporate imprints, can be created in large quantities for special needs. For more information, contact your local bookseller or write to Special Markets, Fodor's Travel Publications, 280 Park Avenue, New York, NY 10017. Inquiries from Canada should be directed to your local Canadian bookseller or sent to Random House of Canada, Ltd., Marketing Department, 2775 Matheson Boulevard East, Mississauga, Ontario L4W 4P7. Inquiries from the United Kingdom should be sent to Fodor's Travel Publications, 20 Vauxhall Bridge Road, London SW1V 2SA, England.

PRINTED IN THE UNITED STATES OF AMERICA

10 9 8 7 6 5 4 3 2 1